A PENGUI

SP

SPOTLIGH

GUY WIN

GUY WINT

SPOTLIGHT

ON

ASIA

PENGUIN BOOKS

Penguin Books Ltd, Harmondsworth, Middlesex
U.S.A.: Penguin Books Inc., 3300 Clipper Mill Road, Baltimore 11, Md
CANADA: Penguin Books (Canada) Ltd, 47 Green Street,
Saint Lambert, Montreal, P.Q.
AUSTRALIA: Penguin Books Pty Ltd, 762 Whitehorse Road,
Mitcham, Victoria

First published 1955

IN MEMORY
T. M.

Made and printed in Great Britain
by The Whitefriars Press Ltd
London and Tonbridge

CONTENTS

5

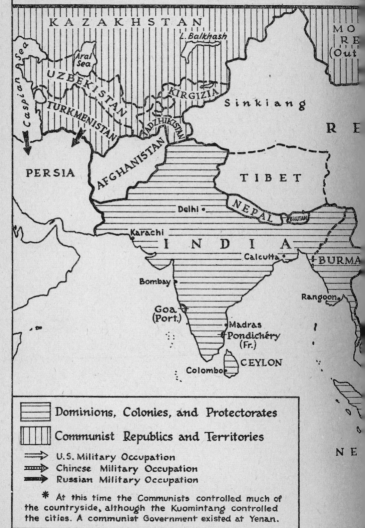

India and the Far East after

Dominions, Colonies, and Protectorates

Communist Republics and Territories

⟹ U.S. Military Occupation
⟹ Chinese Military Occupation
⟹ Russian Military Occupation

* At this time the Communists controlled much of the countryside, although the Kuomintang controlled the cities. A communist Government existed at Yenan.

the Second World War · 1945

MONGOLIAN
REPUBLIC
(Mongolia)

U.S.S.R.

Sakhalin

Manchuria

Maritime Prov.

Kuriles

Inner Mongolia

Vladivostok

Peiping

NORTH KOREA

REPUBLIC

Seoul

SOUTH KOREA

JAPAN

Yenan

Tokyo

OF

Nanking

Hiroshima

CHINA

Shanghai

Chungking

Ryukyu Is.

Okinawa

U.S. Military Occupation

Formosa

Hong Kong (Br.)

Macau (Port.)

Hanoi

HAINAN

INDO

Marianas Is.

AM

CHINA (Fr.)

Bangkok

Manila

PHILIPPINES (U.S.A.)

Guam (U.S.A.)

Saigon

BR. N. BORNEO

Caroline Is.

MALAYA

SARAWAK

Singapore

NETHERLANDS EAST INDIES

Batavia

New Guinea

Austl. Mandate

Papua

Port. Timor

9

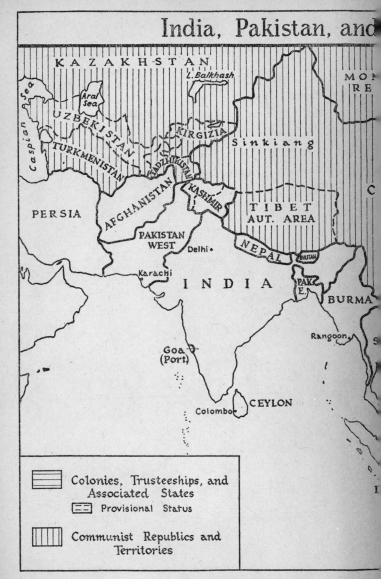

KAZAKHSTAN
L. Balkhash
Caspian Sea
Aral Sea
MON
RE
UZBEKISTAN
KIRGIZIA
TURKMENISTAN
Sinkiang
TADZHIKISTAN
AFGHANISTAN
KASHMIR
PERSIA
TIBET
AUT. AREA
PAKISTAN
WEST
Delhi
NEPAL
BHUTAN
Karachi
INDIA
PAK.
E.
BURMA
Goa
(Port)
Rangoon
CEYLON
Colombo

Colonies, Trusteeships, and
Associated States
Provisional Status

Communist Republics and
Territories

INTRODUCTION

'THE nether sky opens, and Europe is disclosed as a prone and emaciated figure, the Alps shaping like a backbone, and the branching mountain chains like ribs. Broad and lengthy lowlands stretch from the North of France across Russia like a grey-green garment hemmed by the Ural mountains and the glistening Arctic ocean.

'The point of view then sinks downward through space, and draws near to the surface of the perturbed countries, where the peoples, distressed by events which they did not cause, are seen writhing, crawling, heaving, and vibrating in their various cities and nationalities.'

Thus Thomas Hardy, in the prologue to *The Dynasts*, presenting Europe as it was in the year 1805.

The drama which has been played in the continent of Asia during the past few years is not less exciting than that of Napoleon's Europe – or of the struggle against Hitler – though fortunately it has so far not included a major war between the great powers. Asia, in the words of the principal Chinese revolutionary Mao Tse-tung, has 'stood up'. It has ended the ascendancy of the West. For the first time for some centuries it has become again a part of the world on which the historian or philosopher must concentrate if he wishes to see what of lasting interest is happening in this period of the history of man.

Its leading personalities, its ideas and the structure of social life which it is producing, are the main subject matter to be studied in this book. But the compassionate observer will never forget the peoples 'writhing, crawling, heaving, and vibrating in their various cities and nationalities'. That is the stuff of life.

Ex oriente lux. Is there reason to think that Asia, by its political renaissance, will bring new wealth to human life – new conceptions or ways of life, religion or philosophies? It may be so, though it will not necessarily happen. Nevertheless the world's attention is already claimed by the political facts. The overthrow of the Western empires in Asia, their replacement by national states, the retention in some of these of a Western liberal system, the rival system of Communism in Asia, the commanding personality of Asian political leaders, the assertion by Asia of equality with the West – these in themselves form drama enough to draw and hold the interest of those Western countries which until recently had dominated Asia almost without effort.

Suppose an eye like that of Hardy turned upon this spectacle, surveying Asia from outer space and then moving downwards for closer inspection. What, for the best view of the drama, should be the point of time at which the eye first opens, and the place upon which it becomes focused?

The day is 15 August 1947. From a remote distance, Asia appears as a jumble of mountains and deserts, for that is what the greater part consists of. Its population, whose hugeness and multiplication constitute one of the world's most alarming problems, is for the most part crammed into a small number of fertile river valleys, most of them celebrated in history. As the eye travels downwards it rests on this day on Delhi, the capital city of India – the capital from this day no longer of a dependent empire but of a country set free by the dynamic force of nationalism.

At the stroke of midnight between the 14th and 15th of August, Indian independence has been formally proclaimed. The ceremony, which was dramatic, took place in the parliament house. There was an awareness that this was a peculiarly charged moment of history, and many of those taking part in it were conscious that the night's events would be repeatedly described and reviewed by posterity.

> *How many ages hence*
> *Shall this our lofty scene be acted o'er*
> *In states unborn and accents yet unknown.*

Their sense of fate was well-founded; for the Hindu priests in the parliament hall who at midnight blew conch shells to announce the new age were proclaiming more than India's own freedom. In India's emancipation lay, both symbolically and causally, the ending of all the long centuries of Western ascendancy in Asia, the period during which much of Asia was controlled at long range by sea from Europe (as part of America had been controlled by Spain), the period which has been called the Vasco da Gama age in Asia, since it had begun with the arrival of Vasco da Gama and his warships and cannon in the South Indian ports in 1498. Burma, Ceylon, Indonesia, Indo-China – all of which had been parts of this European empire maintained by sea power – must be set free in the train of India. Everybody who could see plain saw this.

In Delhi, which the eye perceives as a strange combination of modern garden suburb and ancient oriental metropolis, the huge crowds move exultantly about the streets. At the Red Fort, once the red-stone citadel of the Moghul Emperors, the centre of the politics of the Indian Mutiny ninety years earlier, the Union Jack has been ceremonially replaced by the new national flag of India, which is based on the flag of the Indian National Congress by whom the independence has been won. The eye would notice one fact with some surprise. Lord Mountbatten, who is laying down the office of British Viceroy in order to become the Governor-General of free India elected by the Indian leaders, is greeted by the crowds with the same enthusiasm as the Indians. In fact he is acclaimed as one of the main actors in the voluntary surrender of British power.

Though there could be no ignoring of the shadows still over India – poverty, hatred, anxiety, disease – and though even on 15 August communal riots were already taking place in the Punjab, within dangerously easy range of Delhi, yet in Delhi on that day there was a temporary amnesia. 'The world's great age begins anew.' That was the mood; and the eye would have had to be prophetic to see the carnage which within a month was to take place in the Punjab as Hindu refugees poured out of the new country of Pakistan and Moslem refugees poured from India.

To most of those who exulted during that August day in Delhi, the dramatic events may have seemed to be a culmination and conclusion of a period. But really they were less an end than the start of a new age. Drama as vivid was to take place in the next few years in all the centres in Asia – in the capitals of the ancient Chinese Empire, Nanking and Peking, in Lhassa, in Rangoon, in Karachi, in Hyderabad, in Jakarta, in Katmandu, in Rawalpindi, in Hanoi, in Goa. Other themes were to be added to the relatively simple one of the fight of nationalism against imperialism.

To discover these themes, to extract from the complex events a narrative of the post-war history in Asia, is the purpose of this little book. It is a review of the 'surface of perturbed countries . . . and of peoples distressed by events which they did not cause'.

NOTE

TO-DAY *the literate people in nearly all Asian countries feel, along with many other sentiments, a sense of belonging to the Asian continent, and therefore of having some kind of interest common to one another. This is natural because during the last century the Europeans during their period of ascendancy thought and spoke of the whole continent of Asia as having a unity – as an entity united by the fact that the whole area was a target for the Western empires. Asia thus became a single concept. Later, as the countries of Asia became emancipated one by one, or, where they had not been actually subject reasserted their equality with the West, as in the case of China, it has been natural again to see Asia's experience as in some sense a unity. All Asia was resurgent; and as each individual country was taking part in a movement extending to the whole continent, all the countries were thus bound together.*

Nevertheless the differences between the different nations and territories in Asia are greater even than in Europe. In history, in ethnology, in language, in religion, in anthropology, the divergences are extremely wide. Communications between the principal Asian countries have in the past been poor; before the last century no principle of Asian unity can be discerned which approached even the very tenuous unity which Europe enjoyed in the concept of Christendom.

These divisions of the past still persist to-day, in spite of the deceptive overlay of pan-Asian feeling. Asia therefore can be analysed intelligently only if it is studied as a number of separate regions – all Asian, but each distinct.

Demarcation of 'natural' regions is always controversial. But Asia to-day divides itself fairly pronouncedly into five great areas–

17

the Indian sub-continent, China, Japan, the South-eastern part of the continent which contains a number of small countries, most of them newly emancipated from Western control, and Central Asia. Of course the borders overlap. But their central cores are the great subject-matter for Asian history.* The shape of their different societies at the time when the Western empires were breaking, and how they had come to take their particular shapes, is the starting point for the study of the Asia of our day. What was the Asia of 1947?

* *Geographically the Arab countries of the Middle East (except Egypt) belong also to Asia. So does Turkey. But recent custom has promoted the Middle East into being almost a continent of its own. Its problems, though they certainly impinge on other Asian countries, are usually treated as distinct from those of the rest of Asia. For this reason the Middle East is not included in this survey.*

PART ONE

Asia in 1947

I

INDIA UNBOUND

MR JAWAHARLAL NEHRU often urges people in the West to recognize how fast Asia is changing. But the change has not begun only in our day. It started with the British occupation of India, which transformed the sub-continent, and created there – in strange contrast with India's past – a liberal civilization. In course of time its political institutions have become those of parliamentary democracy.

The British ruled India for a century and a half. Their achievement, confused and marred though it was bound to be by much that is unedifying in the British record in Asia, has been one on whose account the British name will be remembered in the East. Because of what was done by the British in India a generation or two ago, Britain is still a powerful force in determining Asia's affairs.

During the nineteenth century and the first half of this century, the vast country of India – the centre of the southern part of Asia – had been the most conspicuous example in the world of the subjection of a great country to alien rule. The British Raj was the most impressive of the structures of Western imperialism. India was the largest unit included in the Western empires, the richest, with overwhelmingly the largest population, and with the strongest intellectual and religious traditions.

The British Empire in India was of a pattern rare in world history. Like the Spanish empire in America, it was maintained by sea power operating at a great distance from the home base. It had been made possible by a combination of circumstances, of which two were especially decisive. The first was that India had become relatively backward technically; it had not invented effective artillery or steam-engines, and in particular steam navies. The second was the lesser efficiency, relative to the West, of its social organization. It could not stand up to pressure from outside or rally after shock. Because of these shortcomings India paid the penalty of becoming a country in which the political decisions were made for a long time less by its own people than by outsiders.

Under British rule India went through great and truly revolutionary changes in its entire structure. They were changes in which at least a part of the Indian people acquiesced. To-day, after nationalism has stirred up passion, it is sometimes forgotten that in its first period the British ascendancy was not entirely unpopular. For the Indian governments had collapsed before a civilization which the Indians after a time recognized as more efficiently organized than their own, even if less valuable on other grounds. The more alert members of society concentrated for a long period not upon the recovery of their freedom but on their own transformation and modernization. They exposed themselves voluntarily to the new influences, though selectively. Of course there were conservative groups. But it was not these who made history. The British government therefore for a long while met with co-operation which was almost pathetically willing.

To summarize briefly the changes in India during the British Raj is very difficult. They are too many and too complex. Perhaps it is fairest to leave them to be described by Asians themselves. One of the most remarkable Indians of this generation is Sardar K. M. Panikkar – diplomat, administrator, novelist, poet, and historian. (He came into the glare of world notice when he was Indian ambassador in China at the time of the Korean war, and warned the United Nations, as it proved correctly, about the consequences of crossing the 38th Parallel.) Among a long series of historical books, Panikkar wrote recently a monumental study of the experience of Asia during the age of imperialism.

The first and most abiding change in India he finds in the conception of law. 'The imposing and truly magnificent legal structure under which the people of India lived during the last hundred years has changed the basis of society in a manner which few people realize. A vast corpus of legislation has profoundly affected every kind of social relationship. The position of women in India, for example, has undergone changes which Hindu thought even fifty years ago would have considered revolutionary. ... There can be no going back on this – in any case to the old Hindu ideas. The transformation brought about by the new legal doctrines of the West is a permanent one and is likely to outlast the more spectacular changes in many other fields.' *

That is strongly stated, yet the consequences may be traced even further. One of the results of the rule of law was that power became dispersed. Here is a central fact of modern India. Here is the turning point from the past. In former times, from the dawn of Indian history down to the coming of the British, all power in an Indian state was concentrated in the hands of the King's government. The population lay before his officers as so much material to be controlled and exploited. The very word for an Indian peasant – raiyat – means one of a herd, and the herd implies an owner. Action on his own account by the citizen was usually dangerous, unless it was limited to religious life; wealth in the hands of the citizen was fair plunder for the state. The degree of despotism varied of course from century to century and from region to region; and the sheer difficulty of exerting power, in a land of poor communications and defective organization, saved the population from great excesses, except when it was unlucky. But the fact that all power belonged to the government – that traditional India was totalitarian within the limits of the techniques of the time – explains why there was no political creativeness by the people themselves; why there were no communes or municipalities as in Europe, no multiplicity of societies to promote various public purposes, and, on the whole, no, or at least few, great mercantile corporations.

The introduction of the rule of law changed all. Henceforward government had to act legally; its course was prescribed, its monopoly of power broken. The individual citizen, as long as he acted lawfully, was protected by law.† Thus the rule of law meant

---

* *Asia and Western Dominance*, K. M. Panikkar.

† Of course, nobody could pretend that the courts worked perfectly. Police methods in British India were not those of Britain. The courts did not always succeed in preventing themselves from being deceived.

freedom, and freedom set in motion the energies of the peoples which were to create contemporary India.

Another of the changes which came about under the British Raj was the construction of a civil service superior to any which had been known before in Asia, the Chinese mandarinate not excepted. The British Raj was really governed, not from London or by the viceroy, but by a college of professional administrators, the celebrated I.C.S. In the beginning all its superior members had been British; but by the time that power was transferred more than half the members were Indian, mostly drawn from the new middle class, and a tradition had been created which it was relatively easy to pass on. Even the sternest critics must agree that much of the tradition was good. The civil service was efficient, economical, almost incorruptible, and unflamboyant. The picture of the service as an office-bound bureaucracy is a myth invented by Indian nationalists in their campaigning days (and later admitted by most of them to be unjust); in a sense it was the least bureaucratic of civil services, for its life was in the districts where the administrator regulated affairs with his hands and eyes. One of the excellent features of the service was the tradition that each of its members must take his share of responsibility. A disposition by a junior member to shirk decision and pass responsibility to his seniors was noted as a defect, and might affect adversely his promotion. This habit of dividing responsibility among all officers – each officer being expected to run the affairs of his own district with the minimum intervention from outside – helped to prevent civil-service rule from becoming totalitarian and helped to keep political power in check. Certainly the civil service had defects. Some of its officers were too highhanded, especially in the mid nineteenth century. Some became lethargic or eccentric because they were too little controlled. Some were men of very limited minds. Nearly all lived too much aloof from the ordinary life of society and formed a narrow caste. But all professions in India are apt to turn into castes.

Of course the tradition of civil service was not new in India. Several castes had been devoted to it for many centuries. The whole system of district administration had been built up under the Moghuls and earlier empires. Indian government is a palimpsest; more ancient matter always lies under the contemporary text. But both civil service and the administrative systems took, under the British Raj, a distinctive form which they had not had before.

The changes which resulted from the new freedom in India brought about an entirely new social structure. Some of the traditional classes lost their importance or died out. Generations were born who were confronted with a new chart of what ambitions were legitimate, what patterns of life were admirable, what obligations lay upon them. Guiding themselves by this chart, they changed the face of the country. Great new cities came into being, first as commercial centres, then for industry. An industrial proletariat began to form. But of most importance for the time was the new middle class, large, relatively wealthy, self-confident, ambitious, and to a surprising degree Westernized. It began to feel that it was the destined governing class in India. It was interested in ideas and its mind was fortified by the literature of Europe; British influence fostered on the whole a humanistic outlook rather than the attitude of the technician. A part of the middle class took a liberal view about the place of women, who began to play an animating part in public affairs. It had idealism and a sense of social purpose, being ready (within limits) to put the national welfare above its own sectional interests. It broke away with great success from the quietism which for centuries had condemned many Hindus to inaction – a quietism born partly of political despair, partly of Hindu metaphysics, which had presented such a grandiose spectacle of the cosmic drama and of the aeons of reincarnations before each individual that his life in this particular incarnation had seemed trivial and not worth much effort.

In India and in other oriental countries it is necessary to distinguish a section of the middle class which has had quite exceptional influence. This is the intelligentsia. An intelligentsia is always hard to define; it usually flourishes most where there is a great gap between the mass of the people and the upper strata. Significantly, the term 'intelligentsia' was invented in Tsarist Russia; and, significantly also, the class has existed only imperfectly in Britain. Roughly speaking, the intelligentsia in India were those who had received university education, or higher education,

23

and who were interested in ideas. By far the greater part was recruited from the middle class, and it can therefore be described as a section of this class, though the intelligentsia, because of its traffic with ideas, tended to repudiate the commercial middle class as philistine or conservative. The intelligentsia, though often despised or suspected by the well-to-do in India, proved to be the real agents of change. They have been described as the class which originates, the class which makes history and does not merely suffer it. Congress, the trade unions, the Gandhian movement, and later the Communist Party – all would have been impossible without the leadership of the intelligentsia. They wrote the newspapers, taught in the schools, ran the agitations. They shared the ideals and ambitions of their coevals in the West, though they might oscillate erratically between competing ideals. Confronted with the archaic circumstances of India, they were convinced of the need for drastic change.

There was comedy and pathos in the life of the intelligentsia because though as a class it was so influential its individual members lived usually a harassed existence, in constant anxiety about how to earn their keep. They would discuss how to revolutionize society and bring in a golden age – and then they would go out to scheme how to borrow the next rupee, or to scramble with countless other candidates for miserably paid clerical jobs. For their miserable economic position the government's education policy was partly to blame. It had created universities able to turn out graduates far in excess of the jobs available to them. Not only were the intelligentsia unhappy economically but also psychologically. They had divided minds, and this reflected the contrast between their education and the society in which they lived. The member of the intelligentsia was all for science – yet if he or his family fell sick he was tempted to sacrifice a goat, or wear a charm, or propitiate Kali. He was all for individualism, yet he felt profoundly guilty if he defied his family. He wanted to be Westernized, yet he half believed in an archaic golden age of his ancestors.

The rise of these new classes and the other changes brought about by British rule in India produced in the end the liquidation of the imperial system. Under the British Raj, India developed a political vitality such as it had not before experienced. It went with a new pride in the majesty and achievements of India in the past.* In the great new cities the middle class took to politics with zest and claimed equality with the Westerners. Key posts in the imperial Civil Service passed gradually into Indian control, and later Indian officers began to permeate the Indian Army. Thus, inside the vestures of a colonial system an extremely vigorous new India had come into being.

The new force of nationalism increased this vigour still further. The spread of nationalism to Asia from Europe, where it had already caused so much commotion, was the most fateful single event of the past half century. Much of the rest of this book is about Asian nationalism. In India nationalism supplied the new politically-minded classes with a cause and a fire. Above all, it unified them (just as British rule had unified the country territorially). This was almost a miracle. India is a vast country and, though Hinduism is a unifying force, it had never been sufficient to unite its peoples politically. The caste system divided them, and also language; the census under the British showed 222 languages, of which eleven were major ones. The knitting together in a common loyalty and enterprise of people born in the different regions, speaking different languages and with different history and traditions, was the supreme achievement of nationalism.

From the start the British government had treated Indian nationalism with caution. At home in England nationalism was regarded as healthy and the sign that there was life in a community. Though some British civil servants changed their views radically when they passed through the Suez Canal, others found it went too much against the grain to deplore in India what they applauded in the West. Some had divided minds, anxious to promote what they conceived to be progress while distrustful of India's ability to govern itself. But others were optimists; two of the first organizers of the Indian National Congress were retired British civil servants.

The British Empire in India had always been a peculiar struc-

* The initiative in the rediscovery of India's past had been taken partly by British civil servants, who had turned in their leisure hours, in lonely districts, to scholarly study of the country in which they were working.

ture. It was sustained with a minimum use of force from Britain. The British people and parliament were unwilling that Britain should incur expenditure in its upkeep, or that its retention should require a national effort. The empire reposed therefore on the consent of Indians. But when a series of great nationalist demonstrations showed that in future the British Raj could be maintained only by force, and by a much greater use of force than had ever been contemplated in the past, the British government began to prepare the way for the transfer of its power into Indian hands.

The way was made easier because of the very good fortune that Britain had possessed an Empire which included Anglo-Saxon peoples who very early had demanded, and gained, the right of self-government. The setting up of dominion government in Canada in the middle of the last century proved to be an extraordinarily influential event. Canada provided the pattern which other dependencies in the British Empire could follow, the Asian ones included. Without the model of Canada it is unlikely that Britain would have known how conveniently and elegantly to bring to an end the British Raj in India.

The surrender of power by Britain took place in a number of stages, beginning really in 1919 and culminating in 1947.* At first Indians had been given partial self-government in the provinces; at the end they became sovereign and independent. Progress was punctuated by periodical explosion when nationalism, pressing the pace, organized resistance to government which led to mass repression. The shock caused by the repression would lead to new concessions by government; there would be a brief respite and relaxation of tension; and then the pace would again quicken. The process would have been quicker if it had not been for the hostility which developed in India between Hindus and Moslems, the latter comprising nearly a quarter of the population of the sub-continent. Nationalism fired the Moslems as well as the Hindus, though a little later than it had fused the Hindus into relative unity. The effect upon most Moslems was to convince them that they belonged to a separate nation which consisted of

* It has been said that the main function of the Indian central government during this time was to prepare for the surrender.

Indian Moslems rather than that they belonged to an undivided nation of Indians. They feared that in a self-governing India they would be dominated, and eventually submerged, by the Hindu nation. Therefore, though at the start of the Indian national movement many of the Moslems had participated, they became alarmed as it developed and formed their own separate national movement, which came eventually to demand a separate Moslem state and homeland. Out of this came finally the new state of Pakistan. But to reconcile the Hindus to this, to convince them that Indian self-government was impossible without partition of the sub-continent, was the work of years. It caused the crises between Britain and the Indian Congress in the war years and in the involved negotiations afterwards. The crisis might have continued indefinitely, and perhaps have led to the dreaded full-scale collision between Britain and Indian nationalism, had it not been for the diplomatic skill and resolution of Sir Stafford Cripps and Mr Attlee in imposing a solution.

This was the history on which the politically-minded classes in India looked back as they assumed power in August 1947.

The new governing class, the middle class, inherited the structure of a liberal and parliamentary state; and a large majority desired to keep it in being, though giving it a little more Indian colour. Their minds were dominated by concepts such as liberty, the rights of the subject, the supremacy of law, the authority of the courts. They were minds totally dissimilar to that of Moghul man or of man at any previous period of Indian history. The politicians were the children of the British Raj, now about to fend for themselves.

The new India was dedicated to a proposition – to the proposition that it was possible to govern the country, reform the abuses of its society, and modernize it economically by means of a government which was not authoritarian, which operated according to law, which tolerated a maximum of diversity among its subjects, and which, though attempting to lead, would respect the right of the individual to criticize and, if he chose, to work for a different form of government.

To desire to operate the liberal system was not necessarily to succeed. Success, indeed, would be remarkable, for there are few

27

instances of political institutions being taken over from one society and grafted on to a quite dissimilar one without undergoing radical change. In India, even after the sweeping changes under the British, had society really been transformed sufficiently to make the liberal institutions anything but freakish?

Behind the middle-class suburbs, where power resided, lay the deplorable industrial cities with their proletariat and the vast wastes of the countryside; 83 per cent of the Indian people still lived on the land; 82 per cent were illiterate. What did these care for parliaments, constitutions, law courts, or liberty? What were the ambitions and ideas of even the lower middle class, the class of the clerks and foremen and minor technicians, with whom, as the franchise was extended, the dominant upper middle class would have to come to terms? It was very unlikely that the masses would cherish the same values as the class which had brought India its freedom. If the masses were to show attachment to the new system of government, that system would have to show striking and rapid success.

Most of the leaders of the new independent India understood from the start that their future was very doubtful. But they set themselves with vigour to improve their prospects and strengthen the prospects of the liberal system. True, in the first months after independence there was a moment of anti-climax, of cynicism, and loss of sense of direction. But this passed quickly and the sense of purpose was re-established.

2   CHINA'S PAST

THE civilization of China, throughout the centuries remarkably different from that of India, has been, together with that of India, the great product of Asian history.

The fortunes and evolution of these two civilizations, the Chinese and Indian – which up to the present have interacted surprisingly little except in matters of religion – are the main themes of Asian affairs; all which happens elsewhere in Asia, though it may be of great intrinsic interest, is of subordinate interest.

Like Indian civilization, Chinese civilization was changed profoundly by contact with the West; but because of the deep differences between the two countries, because the pressure of the West operated in different ways, and because of accident, China responded quite differently from India – with consequences which may be fateful for all the world.

Until recently, China's importance in the world has generally been undervalued in the West, except by scholars specializing in its affairs. This has happened because in the latter part of the last century, China was moving into one of the phases of decadence which have often occurred in its history of more than two thousand years; and in the present century it has been passing through almost continuous revolution. Thus it fell into partial contempt. Thirty years ago, who in the West was willing to regard China as a world power, even potentially? But the revolution has ended by bringing China back to the forefront of the world's attention. After the second world war, which in Asia was partly a result of the revolutionary upheaval in the Far East, and still more after the winding up of the Western empires in Asia, the Chinese revolution was to become the chief disturbing event in the Asian continent. Its nature, causes, scope, and consequence are the subject on which all who are concerned with Asia must now concentrate.

China is the largest unified land mass in Asia. Its history has been the most continuous and coherent in the Asian continent. By the start of the Christian era it had evolved a political and social system in advance of any other in the continent; over the centuries it proved the most stable. The degree of China's conservatism can, it is true, be exaggerated. Changes have been constantly taking place. Yet they were like renovations in an ancient house; the house was not pulled down.

The main elements of the system were comparatively simple At the base was the peasantry, better disciplined and mor civilized than the peasantry of any other country in the world. Not that the Chinese peasant was not capable at times of excesses and cruelty; but the constraints imposed by custom were usually effective. Out of the labour of the farmers, out of the taxes taken from them, came eventually all the glories of the Chinese Empire. They bore it on their back.

Above the peasantry came the landed gentry, a very large class and the decisive one in the development of Chinese civilization. Nearly all its members were holders of very small properties; they were not at all like the Prussian junkers or English territorial magnates. A holding of thirty or forty acres was enough to give a man considerable consequence, at least in the richer parts of the country. This gentry of petty landlords governed China. In the villages they were the bosses. They possessed the capital by which agriculture was financed. From their families, and from them almost alone, came the civil servants of the imperial government. They produced the teachers, poets, painters, philosophers. They provided the public opinion of the country.

Although there were at all times large cities in China, the town dweller never enjoyed great influence. Chinese cities were accumulations of people rather than corporations with an institutional life.*

The government was carried on by a corps of professional administrators whose organization anticipated in a curious way the Indian civil service of the British Raj. A college of administrators is nearly always a conservative body; the pressure brought upon the eccentric member can be overwhelming. The Chinese mandarinate was no exception to this rule. Described in such broad terms, the Chinese civil service often sounds decorous and dull. In fact it was always divided by factions whose members felt extreme rancour to one another. The career of almost every civil servant, however distinguished, was punctuated by periods of banishment to remote districts or other punishment such as compulsory suicide.

It has been suggested that one reason why China developed so

---

* For reasons which it is not easy to understand, no industrial revolution occurred in the past in China, though many of the circumstances might have seemed to favour it. The Chinese were inventive and ingenious. There was accumulation of capital. But the revolution did not happen. Thus the country was spared the task of adjusting itself to great changes and accommodating the new social classes which industrialization engenders.

early a bureaucratic civil service was that its agriculture had early become dependent upon irrigation, and that the irrigation system required a bureaucracy in order to administer it. The theory is ingenious, but more study has still to be made of the early history of the canal services in China.

At the summit of the Chinese political system was the Emperor, sitting upon the dragon throne. Some Emperors, by force of personality, could animate the whole sluggard machine of the civil service, and could affect the temper of their time; similarly a bad Emperor, if he chanced to coincide with critical times, could bring his dynasty to ruin and cause upheaval in the country. But the less outstanding Emperors were really very senior civil servants, who combined with their political functions a number of priest-like or symbolic roles. It was held that the entire well-being of the country depended upon the Emperor's virtue. By performing the sacred rites of spring ploughing, the Emperor could make the whole land fertile.

In the course of centuries the bureaucracy became elaborately organized. But no very profound theories of administration were developed. The Chinese were not interested in such ideas as the formal division of power between the centre and localities. Government was paternalist, and the superior government official was always conceived of as the representative of the Emperor, carrying on the administration and admonishing the people like the head of a family.

Restraints upon this bureaucratic government were provided by the pervading ethics and customs – principally Confucian ethics – in which all the corps of bureaucrats were steeped, as well as those whom they governed. Moderation, adaptation to the facts of human nature, a philanthropic if authoritarian system, – these were the characteristics which the Chinese official mind desired to see in government. The instinctive self-control by the bureaucracy proved adequate through the centuries to ensure at most times a comparatively mild government – much milder than in India before the British Raj. A contributing cause was that the government lacked the physical means to maintain a grinding tyranny; China was too huge, communications too primitive, for really effective despotism. Moreover when maladministration went beyond a certain point, the people did not hesitate to revolt. Their right to rebel against bad government was a part of Chinese tradition. Even though the Emperor, as the son of heaven, shared in some form in the divine right of kings, an emperor who misgoverned was held to have forfeited automatically his divine right, and the hand raised against him was not impious, provided that the revolt succeeded.

Traditionally, the individual citizen in China might therefore find life tolerable. But the safeguard of his rights was the moderation of government, not political institutions. In China there was nothing like Roman law, no elaborate codes, no procedures applied inflexibly. Courts were held by executive officers who gave judgements chiefly by common sense. The absence of a legal tradition and a rule of law was to affect profoundly the history of China in our own day.

The pattern of Chinese society stayed relatively unchanged, but Chinese history was not static. It falls naturally into a rhythm of dynastic periods, of which there have been eight since Chinese society took its characteristic shape. A dynasty flourishes and ensures peace. There is a flowering of art and letters. In the shelter afforded by strong government, the population grows. Pressure on the land begins to become heavy. In consequence the size of farms dwindles; distress causes the sale of land, and ownership is concentrated in the hands of landlords. Because of the competition for the land which is available, the landlords can raise their rents. Poverty causes growing disorder throughout the country as a desperate peasantry takes to banditry. The central government weakens. The public doubts the ability of the dynasty to continue. It is said to have 'exhausted its mandate from heaven'. Eventually it either collapses, and is superseded by some new general or chieftain who establishes his power on the ruin of the fallen dynasty, establishing a new dynasty to succeed it, or else it is overthrown by foreign invasion. Sometimes the period of disorder, when a dynasty is collapsing and a new dynasty is struggling to be born, may take decades, and during this time there may be dreadful upheavals and civil war.* The population

* The collapse of central power at the end of the Han dynasty lasted an exceptionally long time.

is reduced and the pressure on the land declines. These conditions favour the restoration of strong government.

This rhythm in Chinese history, of death and rebirth, has been clearly in evidence during the past hundred years. The Manchu dynasty, which had overthrown the Mings in the middle of the seventeenth century, was by the mid nineteenth century ageing fast. Manchus were foreigners, a nomad people from beyond the Great Wall, and though they ruled essentially as Chinese and conformed to the established system, their foreign origin was held against them. The fact that one of the typical periods of nadir in Chinese civilization coincided with the challenge from the West was a great misfortune for the country. It would in any case have been hard for a Chinese government to maintain its authority against Western powers armed with so many weapons of offence. For the Manchus, who in the middle of the nineteenth century were already faltering in dealing with domestic insurrection, the task was hopeless.

The Westerners came by sea – the British and French pushing further east from their positions in the Indian Ocean, the Americans from across the Pacific. Their demand was that they should be allowed to trade freely. The Chinese government, fearing their intentions and the disruptive effects of foreign merchants wandering through the country, tried to keep their ports closed; but the Western navies opened them forcibly. The Chinese coast, and the river valleys, became dotted with colonies of Western business men, living in 'concessions' which the Chinese government had been forced to grant them. The subjects of the Western governments enjoyed extra-territorial rights. Western warships and merchant ships sailed as they pleased along the coast of China and up its rivers.

The spectacle in China at the beginning of the present century was remarkable. In the rural districts the old civilization continued almost unchanged. But in the ports, great new towns arose, chiefly Western in their architecture. Shanghai, the largest of these, was administered – under the supervision of the foreign consuls – by a municipal council elected in practice by the foreign firms. The imperial customs duties were collected by a service organized by foreigners: this had come about because the receipts

were hypothecated for serving foreign loans. Christian missionaries swarmed over the country: to attack them was to provoke punitive expeditions. At Peking all the forms of the imperial government were still preserved; but the government, humiliated by its failure to maintain the national cause against the foreigner, was known to be doomed.

The Western contact with China had two peculiarities. First it insulted the pride of the Chinese, the proudest and most complacent people in the world. For centuries all Chinese had thought of China as the centre of the world, to which barbarians came to bring tribute and proclaim submission, and the shock was therefore the greater when the Chinese encountered a superior strength before which they had to yield. The injuries done to them by the foreigner would not be forgotten until they had been amply avenged. Chinese of all classes fumed, muttered, and longed for redemption. In retrospect the foreign merchant in China appears as almost unbelievably reckless, taunting the Chinese dragon because he believed it dying or dead. The famous notice put up in the park on the bund at Shanghai, 'Dogs and Chinese not admitted', is one example of the follies committed.*

The second peculiarity of the history of the West and China was that in China the West was chiefly destructive, and not simultaneously creative as it had been in India. This came about because the Western governments had not proceeded against China beyond certain limits; they had not annexed its soil, beyond certain small areas, or taken responsibility for its administration. That China escaped conquest, while nearly all South Asia did not, is one of the major facts of nineteenth century history. Partly it was due to the fact that several Western powers were interested in the fate of China – America, Britain, France,

---

* Pearl Buck, in her book *My Several Worlds*, gives an enlightening recollection of games she played as a child in China with the children of her family's servants. 'Our version of the universal game of cops and robbers in those days was the endless war of Chinese and all good Asian allies against the imperial powers of the West. Thus half a century ago did the children of Asia play at the game of later reality.' If her elders in China had given the same attention to what she learned in the market as was given to the youthful Kim at Simla, they might have been better prepared for what was to happen in our day.

34

Russia, and Germany; none could steal a march on the others, and none would permit its rivals to take Chinese territory for themselves unless it made a compensating annexation. Chinese may be glad of their preservation; but the result was that Chinese society never underwent the transformation and regeneration such as had been experienced in India. True, Western trade had given a fillip to the growth of cities and of a class of Chinese traders who enjoyed great prosperity – the so-called compradores, the go-betweens of the foreign merchants and the country as a whole. But there did not come into being a middle class such as made the Congress movement in India.

The Western contacts had, however, brought into being a Chinese intelligentsia. One of the main actions of Western philanthropy in Asia – which limped along actively behind imperialism – was to found universities. From these came a mass of students who had little prospect of employment but who were full of the ideas which in the preceding hundred years had so deeply influenced European civilization. Nationalism, democracy, egalitarianism, liberalism, parliamentarianism, industrialism, socialism, the belief in material progress, and the belief that it was the duty of the state to promote social progress – all these great principles struggled and competed in their minds. The ambition of the intelligentsia was to translate these principles into action and arrest the decay of China. Their tragedy was that they saw no means of obtaining political authority, and felt themselves powerless.

This Chinese intelligentsia, in spite of its zeal, lacked the clarity of mind and also the inquisitiveness of the Indian. Perhaps the Chinese language is unsuitable for promoting exact thought. The writings of this class in the early years of this century are often extraordinarily vague, and their remarks about the outside world were not very penetrating – very much less so than were the observations of Western travellers about China. But in China the intelligentsia were none the less a powerful force bringing about change.

The situation which existed there at the start of the century was thus a revolutionary one. The actual political revolution began in 1911; and it has been continuing to the present day. The start was the overthrow of the imperial government.

3   CHINA'S CIVIL WAR

THE Chinese Empire had been tottering for decades. By ill fortune, in the latter part of the nineteenth century power had passed into the hands of an Empress regent who, though a woman of great determination and skill in intrigue, lacked long-sighted political judgement. She put down the reformers in the imperial service who tried to modernize China by selective borrowing from the West as the neighbouring Japan had been modernized. She governed by means of the conservatively-minded part of the mandarinate. Disaster after disaster in foreign relations brought disgrace upon the government. In 1894 it lost a war with Japan. Corruption became notorious. The funds raised for building a navy with which to fight Japan had been diverted to rebuilding the imperial palace. The Chinese who wanted progress and equality with the West came to feel that their first task was to rid themselves of the monarchy.

At the turn of the century the popular xenophobic movement of a society called the Boxers spread to Peking. Marching in from the country, the Boxers attacked the foreign legations. The imperial government could not check them; some officials encouraged them. The Western governments sent troops to Peking and relieved the legations; the Empress fled to the interior; the government had thus once again lost face. To the observant Westerner this appearance of mass levies of peasant rebels – who were repeating the insurrection four decades earlier of a sect called the Taipings – should have given a warning of the future course of events. Power in China was eventually to pass to whoever could best rouse and organize the peasant masses.

In the confusion following the Boxer rebellion the recruitment for the mandarinate was given up for the first time for centuries. This was an important event. China lost its corps of professional civil servants. One of the elements in Chinese society was disappearing.

In the meanwhile Chinese revolutionaries had formed a number of secret societies working for the overthrow of the imperial government. (Traditionally, secret societies have played a major part in Chinese politics.) One of the chief of these societies was the body which was eventually to become the great nationalist party, the Kuomintang. Its leader was Dr Sun Yat-sen; and its funds came from Chinese who had settled and prospered in the United States and in south-east Asia. During the early years of the century there had been a number of plots against the government, which failed. In 1911, after the old Empress had died, the secret societies at last succeeded. A revolt was started at Hankow. It was not well planned. By all reasonable expectation it should have failed. But at its signal the imperial administration in city after city collapsed like wood long rotten. Its generals and officials betrayed it or were killed. The Manchu garrisons, which were stationed throughout China, were massacred by popular rising. The Emperor abdicated. Thus another of the elements in Chinese society disappeared. China, some parts of which for 3,000 years had known a Son of Heaven upon the Dragon Throne, became a republic.

Who was to hold power in the new republic? The revolution had been made in the name of democracy. In 1911 it was taken for granted by revolutionaries everywhere that after every revolution a parliamentary government should be set up. A parliament was therefore convened at Peking. But Dr Sun Yat-sen and his party, whose organization except as a secret society was rudimentary, was unable to establish a government. Power passed to the military, to the remnants of the old imperial army. But the army, like the rest of the empire, did not hold together. Local commanders, even if giving nominal allegiance to Peking, became independent. Soon, as a result of the growing confusion, they encountered as competitors a number of bandit commanders who had risen to power by raising bandit armies.

This state of affairs continued for nearly fifteen years. The intelligentsia of China, the products of the new universities which flourished in spite of the political chaos, were in despair. This period was brought to an end when Dr Sun Yat-sen, who had established himself with the help of a friendly general in a small area round Canton, appealed for aid to Moscow. The Russians sent him Michael Borodin. This man had a strange history. He had begun life as an engineer and emigrated from Russia to America, where he prospered. After the Russian revolution he returned to Moscow. His mission to China lasted only a short time, but during it he became an international celebrity, filling the non-Communist world with deep apprehension. He was to return to Russia more or less in disgrace and to spend the remaining twenty years of his life in obscurity, dying as one of Stalin's prisoners in a concentration camp.

He conceived it to be his task to reorganize the Kuomintang, no longer as a party prepared to take part in parliamentary politics, but on the same lines as the Communist party in Russia, so that it might become a well-disciplined political force able to establish its authority because it was more efficient than any of its rivals. He wanted to make the Kuomintang the General Staff of the Chinese Revolution. A good account of his work was given at the time by a correspondent of the *Manchester Guardian* who had an interview with him at Canton:

'Borodin himself would not claim any special gifts as the commanding personality attributed to him by those who do not understand that what was important was not the man but the things he had to say. Borodin may properly be considered as a good gramophone. He was important because the sole record that was sent with him was precisely the record that Dr Sun Yat-sen needed to hear. That record is the twenty years' experience of the growth and struggles of the Bolshevik party in Russia ... Borodin had to teach a *bourgeois* revolution the methods of revolution in general as tested in practice during the last quarter of a century in Russia.'

The correspondent gave a vivid personal sketch of Borodin as he appeared at this time:

'Borodin is a stoutly built man of forty, with a good deal of humour, an excellent knowledge of English (the language through which he communicates with the Chinese), a downright manner of talking, and, when he talks of the Chinese, very much the attitude of mixed admiration, laughter, and annoyance which seems to become that of most foreigners who have much to do with them. On the subject of the outcry made about him, he said: "What is all the fuss about? The institution of advisership in China is a very old one. It is not my fault, nor Russia's fault, that England did not help Sun Yat-sen. There was Sun expecting, with his boundless good faith, that the countries which had taught him his Utopian idea of democracy would lend him a helping hand. They called him a lunatic. Well, I came to Canton on a voyage of discovery, and found Dr Sun Yat-sen in very great difficulties. I took off my coat and settled down to help him in that horrible tropical climate, with insects of a size and ferocity I had never known in Russia, no snow, no winter, and the sweat dripping on my papers. Horrible it was, loathsome, and now that Dr Sun is being proved to have been not such a lunatic after all, you people turn round and curse me for doing what you might have done yourselves. It is not what you can call sportsmanlike".'

The fatefulness of Borodin's mission in China was that he established in the country the idea that the only form of political party which could hope to master the anarchy was one which was rigidly disciplined like an army. It was a party bent on achieving power at all costs and, once power was achieved, on continuing to hold power at all costs. It was a party which demanded full-time devotion and activity from its members, while insisting that this activity should be exactly according to instructions from a directing authority at the centre. A political party conceived in this way was quite different from the political parties in parliamentary states such as had hitherto been accepted as providing the model for China. For the political party in Britain or America does not demand that its members should surrender themselves to it body and soul: it considers that it has a respectable function to perform in opposition as well as in government; it is run by its members, it does not run them; it thinks it proper to obey certain rules of the political game and, in return for being tolerated by its competitors, is willing to tolerate them.

Once the authoritarian party had been accepted as the form for the future in China, the divergence of China from the path taken by India was accomplished. China, whatever the merits of the system it might adopt, could not become a liberal state. All that was left to be settled was whether the party which established the new state was to be the Kuomintang – which, though reorganized on the pattern of a Communist party, was anti-Communist in its policies – or some rival organized in the same way but pursuing different ends.

It is of course arguable that only a party organized on the authoritarian model could have saved China from chaos and restored a central government. Certainly the parties which followed the Western line did nothing; certainly also the Kuomintang after its reformation entered on a period of surprising success. It was the most efficient organization in China, even if by Russian standards it was still a haphazard body, and even if its army, though no longer simply the personal following of a general, was still in many ways primitive. In its new form it attracted the hope and support both of business men and the intellectuals, who saw in its success the best prospect of ending China's period of anarchy. Within two years of Borodin's reforms the armies of the Kuomintang had defeated all the principal generals in China. A central government had been established which could claim that its authority was recognized, to a greater or lesser extent, in almost every province in the country.

But China's revolution was still not ended. It had scarcely entered even the middle stage.

The task which the Kuomintang was expected to fulfil was to break down the inertia of Chinese society and to modernize it. It was destined to be in the centre of the stage for twenty years, and during that time it accomplished many notable things. It built a large network of more or less modern roads over most of the country. It carried out large-scale hydraulic works and undid some of the damage to the irrigation system which was the result of years of neglect. It made agriculture more profitable by improving the strains of cotton and by reviving sericulture. It fostered a modern banking system. It made intelligent use of the help offered by the technical organizations of the League of Nations. These positive achievements of the Kuomintang have been forgotten because of its subsequent ill fame and because the Communists have been able to obliterate the memory of them. But in the reform of society, in the combating of injustice, and in the evolution of an acceptable political system the Kuomintang failed.

It was not only poverty which made China discontented and explosive. It was the universal injustice and brutality. There was not organized brutality by the government, like that of the Nazis in Germany, but there was the licence of a decaying society without firm government, in which jungle conditions prevailed, and the strong man, whether landlord, village boss, government or party official, army officer or bandit, preyed on the weak. In the villages the landlord, because of the breakdown of the old tradition of government, had been able to increase his exactions, and sometimes would high-handedly confine defaulting tenants in his cellars. As a rule, there was nobody to interfere, because the magistrate was the landlord's friend. Taxes might be levied fifty years in advance; cases were reported where they had been raised ninety years in advance. Outside the coastal cities there was virtually no restraint upon the industrial employer. Investigators of the League of Nations reported a grotesque and appalling rate of mortality among child labourers in the tin mines of Yunnan because no proper protection was given them in their dangerous occupation; but nobody intervened.

China was thus a society urgently in need of reforming measures and an authoritative hand, and these the Kuomintang failed to supply. What was the use of its road building when the most urgent need was a revived social justice and security in the villages? The League of Nations advisers who had been lent to Chiang Kai-shek repeatedly urged upon him the need for reforming measures, and in particular for a reform of rural tenancy. But since the Kuomintang was supported by and needed the landlords, it would take no steps. That was its greatest failure.

To the end the Kuomintang remained a narrow party dictatorship. There was no genuine effort to introduce a democratic system in which the opposition might by constitutional processes replace the Kuomintang. None of the political institutions of the modern world which China might have wished to copy were successfully imported. The Kuomintang did not build up the prestige of the judiciary or establish the rule of law.

The Kuomintang's failures were due partly to the fact that it never established its authority fully and never ended the civil war. At the moment when it was establishing its authority in Central China the party split.

Up to this stage the Kuomintang had included within itself the infant Communist party. This, born out of the ideas set afoot by the Bolshevik revolution, had been founded in Shanghai in 1922.

41

It was inaugurated at a secret meeting in a girls' school in the French concession. (In Russia the Bolshevik revolution was planned at a meeting in the girls' school at Smolny.) From the start the Communists had been divided on tactics – whether to support wholeheartedly the Kuomintang revolution as a preliminary to eventual Communist revolution or whether to try to seize exclusive power for the Communists. As the fortunes of the Kuomintang improved, so the tension grew between the orthodox section of the party and the Communists. To the Communists it became clear that the main power in the party was firmly held by the rural gentry and the Shanghai business men. The secession or expulsion of the Communists became inevitable.*

The rupture came about in April 1927 when Chiang Kai-shek, after the Kuomintang armies had gained control of the Yangtze valley and had taken Nanking and Shanghai, turned upon the Communist-led workers' organizations in Shanghai. There were massacres and executions, which were repeated in other main centres. The Communist leaders who escaped went into hiding. But in Kiangsi a small section of the army declared for the Communists, rebelled, and took to the hills. So began the Chinese Red Army.

This was the beginning of the long civil war between the Com-

* The early history of the Communist Party in China is obscure, partly because most of the Communist records perished (some during the Long March), partly because the Communists have from time to time faked the history. Partly, too, it is because nobody at the time thought of writing down the facts, or had time to do so. This recalls the remarks of the Jesuit missionary Ricci in the sixteenth century on the beginnings of the Christian missionary enterprise in China. 'It not infrequently happens that the beginnings of vast expeditions and mighty undertakings which have matured in the course of ages are all but a closed book to those who live long'after these events. After frequently pondering over the reasons for this fact I came to the conclusion that the beginnings of all events, even of those which later took on vast proportions, were so very small and meagre at the outset that they seemed to give no promise whatever of developing later into anything of importance. Perhaps too it might be preferred to explain this fact by saying that the beginnings of such undertakings were beset with so many and such great difficulties, that we would be warranted in assuming that the authors of these happenings, who were straining every nerve to accomplish their tasks, found but little time and had but little energy left for keeping records of what was happening.'

munists and the Kuomintang, which in the end was to bring the Kuomintang into its final defensive position at Formosa, and which even now is not finished. At first the Communists could make little progress. The leaders put their main hope in organizing revolution by conspiracy in the large cities. The tactics were foolish. Even if they succeeded in seizing a city, they could be crushed by anti-Communist armies marching in from outside. This was shown to be true when they had seized Canton in December 1927. They did better when they shifted the centre of their activity from the towns to the country. In the general lawlessness of China the peasantry had been suffering more and more. They were ripe for an appeal by a revolutionary party which preached class war and promised to divide out the land of the landlords. By this promise they were able to raise large peasant armies with which to challenge the armies of the Kuomintang. The change of tactics was due to Mao Tse-tung, who thereby established his pre-eminence in the Communist party.*

This union in China of the intelligentsia – who supplied the Communist leaders – and peasantry was to be fateful for Asia. At the base of all the Asian societies is the peasantry. How easy it is to forget that the great mass of the people of Asia are still peasants, and that the history of Asia is really their history. Wherever the gaze turns in the continent – to the North Indian plains, to the valleys of China, to Japan – there the peasant is found, anxiously getting his living, usually from overcrowded land, usually by relatively primitive methods of agriculture. A shockingly large amount of his produce is taken from him by the moneylender as interest on the capital he has borrowed, by the landlord as rent, by the state as taxes, by the trader as profit for marketing his crop. Upon the peasants all the rest in Asian society have lived from time immemorial.

'They shall not be sought for in publick counsel nor sit high in the congregation. They shall not sit on the judges' seat, nor

---

* In a report to the party made in 1927 Mao wrote, 'If we allot ten points to the accomplishment of the democratic revolution, then the achievement of the urban dwellers and the military units rates only three points, while the remaining seven points should go to the peasants in their rural revolution.'

understand the sentence of judgement. They cannot declare justice and judgement. But they will maintain the state of the world.'

Resentment by the peasant against his wrongs was not new in China, or in other Asian countries. Periodically there had been jacqueries and bandit risings which had been exploited sometimes to help found new imperial dynasties. But the Communists were the first to make the movement of protest into a political movement by means of which to establish a new form of society.

The Communist peasant armies occupied at first a mountainous tract of country on the borders of Kiangsi and Fukien provinces. Here they defeated five expeditions sent against them by the Kuomintang. They showed baffling skill in guerilla warfare. Their tactics were summed up in the maxim of Mao Tse-tung:

> When the enemy advances, we retreat.
> When he escapes, we harass.
> When he retreats, we pursue.
> When he is tired, we attack.

They carried on ruthless war against the landlords. In 1931 they proclaimed a Chinese Soviet Republic and published their laws. In 1935, finding the pressure of the Kuomintang too strong, they migrated in a mass movement, broke through the cordon of government troops, and by an extraordinary feat of endurance marched over 6,000 miles, first into the far west of China as far as the Tibetan borderland, and then up through the Moslem areas of the north-west into the remote northern part of the province of Shensi. They crossed eleven provinces, and claim to have engaged and defeated 401 regiments of the Kuomintang on their way. Finally they found safety near the Ordos desert, where they set up a capital in the small town of Yenan. The surrounding country consisted of loess hills, and for years the Communist forces lived in caves scooped out of the hill-side. From this centre they could gain new recruits for their depleted forces. Of 100,000 men who began the Long March only 20,000 survived. The Communists had to begin again in building an army.

The Long March had a great effect upon the Communist fortunes. It made the Communists romantic. It was in any case a remarkable military achievement. But also it lent itself to the

Chinese imagination because much of the romantic literature of China – the literature read avidly as a light relief to the rather tedious classics – is about hardy and audacious bandits defying corrupt governments from mountain retreats. The Chinese Communists thus established themselves as an authentic Chinese force. From this time also dates their appeal to the intelligentsia who, except for a small group of doctrinaires such as Mao Tse-tung himself, had hitherto been more repelled by the Communist barbarities than attracted by their promises of reform.

To broaden the bases of support, the Communist leaders while in Yenan moderated their land programme. To those of the possessing classes in their territory who would submit quietly to their rule, they offered indulgence. In their war with the Kuomintang they began to concentrate more on challenging the Kuomintang for its inadequacy in championing the national cause against foreign enemies, especially Japan.

Japan had come to dominate all the politics of China. The rise of Japan was one of the prime facts of the modern history of Asia. Alone of Asian countries, Japan proved able to borrow enough of the techniques of the West to compete with the Western countries upon equal terms. It also joined with the Western countries in becoming an imperialist power. But in stealing a march in this way on China, most of the leaders of Japan recognized that their position was precarious. Traditionally, China had overshadowed Japan. It was very much larger, and had a much larger population, and its civilization was more sophisticated. Throughout the centuries, Japan had been the borrower from China. The Japanese knew that if China could recover from confusion, and could develop modern industry, the old supremacy of China would soon be restored.

They were resolved to prevent this from happening. Before the rise of the Kuomintang, they had been able to dictate to the contending politicians and generals in North China. The growing strength and prestige of the Kuomintang government was a danger sign. From 1927 Japan began a series of hostile acts against it. In 1931, when it looked as if the Kuomintang was about to extend its authority effectively over Manchuria, the Japanese overran that territory and set up a puppet government. In the next few years they alternated between threat of similar action in other parts of China, and blandishments intended to draw the Kuomintang into an exclusive alliance with Japan, which would remove the Western powers from East Asia. In 1937 there began full-scale war between Japan and China, though neither side declared war on the other nor admitted officially that war was taking place.

This war was another great convulsion in China's life. The Kuomintang government was driven back into the far west of the country. Some of its leaders seceded, and organized a pro-Japanese government in the coastal areas; they still claimed to represent the Kuomintang and invoked the name of Sun Yat-sen. But the true Kuomintang, in the words of its leader Chiang Kai-shek, had exchanged space for time. In the remote mountain province of Szechwan, where it was more or less out of reach of the Japanese, it could wait, maintain its authority, and maintain its being – even if a frail one – until Japan's ambitions should bring Japan into collision with the Western powers. This event happened in 1941. By the summer of 1945, Japan was ruined, and the Kuomintang could return to the coastal areas.

In the meanwhile, during the period of exile in Szechwan, the struggle between the Kuomintang and the Communists had continued. Nominally, they had made a truce at the start of the war, and formed an alliance in defence of the country. Public opinion compelled them to do this. The Communists even allowed their army nominally to be incorporated in the Kuomintang forces. But neither the Communists nor the Kuomintang trusted the other. The Communists, while proclaiming through their propaganda great successes in guerilla warfare against the Japanese, carefully limited the amount of fighting which they did. Their interest lay in conserving their force, in adding to it by obtaining as many arms as they could on the pretext that they were to be used against Japan, and in encouraging the Kuomintang patriotic ally to exhaust itself.

The interest of the Kuomintang lay in countering these plans, and, without actually renewing the civil war against the Communists – which would have been condemned by the Kuomintang's friends in the West who wanted all Chinese to collaborate with one another against Japan – in sapping, blockading, and harrying the Communists in their strongholds.*

When Japan collapsed, there was a race by the Kuomintang and the Communists to occupy the best positions in the territory which the Japanese gave up. Thanks to American ships and aeroplanes, the Kuomintang were able to secure Manchuria. But when the dust settled, the Communists were formidably placed, even though they still did not occupy any of the great cities. They had gained control of territory which contained about one-quarter of the total population of China, and from this had organized an army of nearly one million men. Their armament had improved, for when the Japanese in Manchuria surrendered to the Russians, Russia before withdrawing handed many of their weapons to the Communists.

Throughout 1946 attempts were made by America to bring the Kuomintang and the Communists together in a coalition government. America had not yet recognized the true nature of Chinese Communism. There had been effective propaganda to represent the Chinese party as different from the Russian. Communists in China, it was said, were no more than land reformers or Jeffersonian democrats. Their partnership with the Kuomintang was essential if a strong, stable China was to be built up.

The American mediation failed. Neither the Communists nor the Kuomintang really desired that it should succeed. They knew that their struggle was one to the death. There had been intermittent fighting, and by August, 1947 – the date of Indian independence – the civil war had been resumed on a full scale.

During these long domestic struggles in China, the power of China had ceased to be exerted externally. The control of the central government had been precarious over the provinces of China proper. It become practically non-existent in the remoter parts of the Chinese Empire, such as Sinkiang and Tibet. The countries on its periphery which once had acknowledged its suzerainty, such as Indo-China and Nepal, ceased to send envoys and token tribute to Peking.

* On two occasions, in 1938 and 1941, there was serious fighting between Kuomintang forces and the Communist armies.

Chinese majesty and power had been almost forgotten. It had passed into history.

The countries of South Asia, when in 1947 and the succeeding years they became independent, did not realize that the convulsion in China was nearing its end, and that out of it was very soon to emerge a reconstituted central authority which the rest of Asia would have to take into account almost in every act.

'The word of the Lord came unto Jeremiah a second time saying, "What seest thou?" And Jeremiah said, "I see a seething pot, and the face thereof is towards the north." Then the Lord said unto Jeremiah, "Out of the north an evil shall break forth upon all the inhabitants of the land". '

An inspired prophet in South Asia might in 1947 have used much the same words.

4

JAPAN

JAPAN, though it has a history quite distinct from China's, and a strong individuality, forms a part of the Far Eastern region. Japan was one of the chief architects of Asia as it existed in 1947. Perhaps in the future Japan will play a less decisive part – though this is not certain – than it did in the first half of the present century. But for some decades before 1947 it had acted with effects disproportionate to its own size and population.

China is a land empire: Japan an island country on the edge of a continent. (Analogies between its geographical position and Britain's have been persistently pointed out by those wishing to promote good relations between the two countries.) Japan has owed to China a great deal of its civilization, but not, except in inessentials, its political institutions. In Japan in its past history there existed no such corporation of professional civil servants as in China. Traditionally the governing class was a semi-military one. Japan's system of government bore some resemblance to the feudal system of medieval Europe; some people have overstated the similarity, and the Japanese system was peculiar and unique; but the parallel was close in that the political nexus of the upper classes was a tie of reciprocal loyalty between overlord and client.

From the ninth century, the Emperor had been forced into seclusion, and the chief authority in Japan was the shogun, an officer who was the hereditary prime minister.* The rise and fall of the dynasties of shoguns had in Japan the significance of the rise and fall of imperial dynasties elsewhere.

Japan's great achievement in the last century was to withstand more effectively than any other Asian power the impact of the West. It did so because it was the quickest to transform its society to meet the challenge, and the quickest to copy Western technique. This was possible partly because Japan was a maritime country with easy communications. Ideas and commands passed rapidly; the government could more easily maintain its authority. Another cause was that the ruling class was hidebound by no conservative doctrines such as those of Confucius in China. Indeed one of its traditions was to copy freely the institutions of the foreign countries with which it came in touch. It has carried this on to the present day.

The sudden rise of Japan in the second half of the nineteenth century caused the more surprise because for the previous two hundred years the Japanese shoguns had decreed for it an eccentric hermit condition. Earlier, in the sixteenth and early seventeenth centuries Japan had been exposed to Portuguese missionaries and maritime adventurers; and its government's response to the fears which they had aroused was to impose a seclusion upon the country. Japan became a mysterious land. Art flourished; life was lived with curious ceremony. Internally this was one of the most peaceful periods in Japanese history, even though there was economic distress. Nothing prepared the outer world for the spectacular military history on which Japan, once brought back into world society, was about to start.

The degree of Japan's seclusion can be exaggerated. A Dutch merchant settlement was tolerated throughout the hermit period,

* The title, which means literally 'Barbarian – suppressing general', dates in this special sense from the twelfth century.

though its residents were strictly controlled, and were systematically humiliated, for example by being made to trample occasionally upon the Christian cross. A class of Japanese scholars kept themselves fairly well informed about life in the West. Dutch books were one of the mediums through which news was carried. Nevertheless Japan was virtually removed from the world stage as an actor. If it had not been for this self-imposed exile from world politics, Japanese sailors, who were adventurous, might have colonized the Western coasts of America before the European settlers had arrived there.

Japan's seclusion became irritating to the Westerners of the nineteenth century, hungry for trade and conquest.

Its ports were at length re-opened to the West in 1854 as the result of a display of force by an American naval expedition led by Commodore Perry. The account of his mission, written by members of his staff, is very diverting. Psychologically Commodore Perry resembled in a striking way General MacArthur, who was to rule Japan for five years nearly a century later. The necessity of submitting to Perry's demands caused deep resentment in Japan. Some students have suggested that it led to the creation of a national neurosis, which eventually impelled Japan to a vindictive retaliation at Pearl Harbor.

This may be fanciful. Yet the history of Japan cannot be understood without constantly reflecting on the very strange psychology of the Japanese people. They are energetic, macabre, artistic, humourless (though they like horse-play), unintellectual, and highly emotional. Only those Japanese who have been touched by the humane and humorous influences of China – and a few in modern times who have submitted to the influence of the West – show tolerance and moderation. They have been mellowed by Buddhism; but the rival religion in Japan, Shintoism, lacks the large ideas of the greater faiths; it is a mixture of reverence for the state and, at the lower levels, animism. The typical Japanese has often been attracted to courses which shock cosmopolitan man. The guiding force has often been a kind of perverted aestheticism which sees beauty, or at least decorum, in actions which to a more balanced mind show neither of these qualities. Because of the absence of an intellectual tradition, Japanese, when confronted with new situations in which instinctive ways of action are not appropriate or successful, are often at a loss what to do, and take refuge in an outburst of violence.

When Japan was dragged out of seclusion, it was supposed that it would not be long before it passed into the same subordination to the West as other countries in the East, but the West was to find that it had caught a Tartar. For a time Japan was compelled to grant extra-territorial rights to the Westerners. There followed a great convulsion in Japanese society. In 1868, the shogun was overthrown, the shogunate abolished. A group of young men, all ambitious and energetic and some exceptionally able, seized power, and restored in name the political authority of the Emperor, while in fact holding it for themselves. Most of the leaders in this movement came from the lower ranks of the military aristocracy. Empirically minded, they were willing to try rather uncritically almost any device which seemed likely to put Japan in a better competitive position with the Western intruders. Under their government the social and political system of Japan was recast; and few stopped to ask what the ultimate end was to be. A modern army and navy was created, a modern industry, an educational system. Political institutions were copied from Imperial Germany, including a parliament copied from the Reichstag. In an astonishingly short time, the government was strong enough to abolish the privileges which had been extorted by the Westerners.

From that, Japan passed to the counter-attack – and still without much thought of ultimate goals or the rationality of its course. It built the foundations of an Empire by annexing Formosa and Korea. In 1905 it challenged Russia which was threatening to establish its control over Manchuria. The imperialism of an Asian country was pitted against Western imperialism; and Japan won.

It over-reached itself. The nineteen-twenties had been a comparatively calm period, and the parliamentary parties tightened their hold on the government, though the hold was still not complete. During the thirties Japan suffered stresses and strains in its economic system. With a population which was growing rapidly, and which it could not feed, it depended for existence upon its export trade. Its position was curiously like that of Britain. Japan was therefore especially threatened by the world economic depression. To counter this, it practised export subsidies and other measures of 'dumping'. This caused political bitterness against Japan. One section of the leaders in Japan became convinced that Japan, in its economic predicament, could only find safety by obtaining political control of large areas overseas, from which it could then ensure supplies of food and raw materials and whose markets it could control. This group coalesced naturally with the extreme nationalists and militarists who had survived from the past stage of Japanese history.

This led to the convulsions in Japanese affairs. Power passed into the hands of the service leaders and the leaders of the extreme nationalist societies. The parliamentary parties continued in being but politicians had to conform to the current mood. Those who did not were assassinated. The Emperor was pushed into the background, as in the days of the shogunate. There followed an increasingly aggressive foreign policy – the war with China – alliance with Germany and Italy – Pearl Harbor – war against all the Western world, and the eventual destruction by America of the navy, the army, Tokyo – and finally the use of the atom bomb.

Japan's prostration in 1945 was as impressive as had been its power in the years preceding. Japan's pressure, and the threat of an expanding Japanese empire, had been one of the key circumstances in Asia. Suddenly the pressure ceased. The countries which Japan had subjected – Korea, Formosa, and Manchuria as well as those it had acquired in South-east Asia during the war – were suddenly freed. Was Japan to be permanently out of action as a great power? American occupation, far from being punitive, had as its aim the nursing of Japan back to life and strength, though it was hoped to wean Japan from militarism and imperialism. Its future, at the fateful year 1947, was still obscure.

Amid all this dramatic history, Japanese society had of course undergone changes. Though a military spirit still prevailed, the old semi-feudal organization disappeared. A large industrial proletariat grew up. As in India and China, a dissatisfied intelligentsia appeared upon the scene. Ideas from the West poured in. But Japan moved in no settled direction. The impression which it gave was of endlessly experimenting, tasting, testing, being attracted first by one model, then by another. The causes of change were external rather than within itself. Japan's destiny would be made by the influences which it came under.

Partly because of this, the rise and fall of the Japanese Empire, though spectacular, left behind little of permanent worth. The empire makers had been impelled forward by economic causes and by lust for conquest, inherited from an ancient military society. Its imperial expansion, unlike that of most similar instances in modern times, was not associated with original intellectual or moral ideas about how the affairs of humanity ought to be regulated. The attempts made to give the Empire an intellectual justification were grotesque. Japanese publicists claimed quite baldly that it was the natural order of the universe that all peoples should be subordinated to the Japanese Emperor. But why this should be they could not explain. The official doctrines were summed up in an extraordinary little book called the *Kokutai No Hongi – Cardinal Principles of the National Entity of Japan* – compiled by a group of professors in 1937. Over two million copies were sold. In the woolliest of language this expounded the dogma of the Emperor's divinity, absurd myths of ancient Japanese history, the mission of Japan to expand, and the need for discipline. It was distressing that people outwardly so well able to master twentieth-century life should affect to believe so much primitive nonsense as was contained in the legends which were given official sanction.

These are barren facts. But in the mind of the rest of Asia these shortcomings of Japan were modified by the recollection that in 1941 it was Japanese armies which gave some of the countries of South-east Asia their first taste of liberation from Western rule. Japan's claim, first made in 1905, to have been the first to champion Asia against the West, received by these acts a little reinforcement, even if the motive for them had been machiavellian.

THE fourth region is South-east Asia. This is a group of small countries which from early times have been usually under the influence, and sometimes political control, of the great giants, India and China. These countries – Burma, Siam, Indo-China, Malaya, Indonesia, and the Philippines – are the Balkans of Asia.

During the period of Western ascendancy all these countries, except Siam, passed under the control of the Western empires. The Dutch ruled (and until recent times grossly exploited) Indonesia; Burma was a part of the British empire; the sultans of Malaya became British vassals; the Philippines, which had been a Spanish colony since the seventeenth century, was in 1901 taken from Spain by America; the countries which compose Indo-China became protectorates of France.

The political and social civilization of these countries before they fell into subjection had been fairly uniform, in spite of there being no uniformity in religion. Malaya and Indonesia were Moslem; Burma, Siam, and Cambodia and Laos (which formed part of Indo-China) were devoutly Buddhist; Annam was in part – and rather superficially – Confucian. But, whatever the religion of the country, despotic kings or sultans presided over it; tyranny was, however, mitigated by the fact that most of the government which concerned the ordinary subject was carried on by local headmen, who were often hereditary and whose actions were rather strictly controlled by precedent and public opinion. Annam, which was the most under Chinese influence, had a rather more sophisticated form of government than the others; the administration was a half imitation of China's, and the Emperor of Annam carried on at his court the rites copied from Peking.

Western government did not have the same constructive results in South-east Asia as in India. It might have been expected that in the parts of the region which came under Britain there would have been repeated the same feats of political and social architecture which Britain had carried out in India. But of these parts Burma was under British rule for too short a time; upper

Burma was not annexed until 1885. There had not been time enough for a strong middle class to come into being as in India; moreover, its economic basis was lacking, for it was Indian immigrants, not the Burmese, who developed profitable business in Burma. Britain failed in practice to open the civil service to Burmans as it had opened it to Indians. The other British territory, Malaya, was socially and politically the most backward in the area; when it was taken over most of it was jungle. Thus the British political creativeness never really operated in South-east Asia. The other imperial countries – America excepted – governed their empires with different ideas from Britain. They saw no obligation to start on the strange and hazardous experiment of transplanting Western institutions and ideas into Asia. For example, the Dutch in Indonesia aimed at keeping as much of the old order as possible while establishing over it the general control of Dutch administrators. Thus Indonesia was shielded from the forces of the changing world; old institutions were conserved; nothing happened in Indonesia compared with the kaleidoscopic changes brought about in India when the British allowed the winds of the new age to blow unimpeded over it. At the time some observers held this for a virtue, since the life of the Indonesian people was not turned on its head, but in retrospect it appears that it might have been better for Indonesia if it had experienced more of the harsh winter. Changes had to come, and those who had experienced them were in the best position to stand on their own feet when the age of Western ascendancy was over.

The main effect of Western rule in South-east Asia was really to take the region out of world politics and to sever temporarily the links between its countries and the outside world, except for the colonial powers. It became a secluded area, even though it was quite easy to travel there, and it was forgotten except by the experts and the business men. Sardar K. M. Panikkar caused quite a stir when in the latter years of the war he published a book on the region, claiming that its problems would be among the most difficult after the restoration of peace. It was he who first suggested that the countries had common features and, taken together, formed a natural region. 'South-east Asia', an expression heard so often since, was his invention.

Nationalism appeared in the region rather later than elsewhere. It received its first fillip from the economic adversities of the great world depression. Adversity has indeed been the making of the ultimate triumph of nationalism, for the second fillip came in the second world war. After Pearl Harbor, Japan overran the entire region. Its motives were imperialist and many of its acts were much more arbitrary than those of the European rulers, but in spite of themselves the Japanese acted as emancipators. They ended by setting up governments drawn from the leaders of the nationalist movements which even in the backwater atmosphere of South-east Asia had come to life. When the Japanese lost hope of maintaining their empire they proclaimed their puppet governments independent and, perhaps with a shrewd consciousness that they would thereby be robbing the victors of the chance of restoring their former empires and of reverting to the position before Japan's turbulent outbreak, they gave out to the nationalists the arms which they themselves could no longer use.

Even after this the liquidation of the Western empires did not come about overnight. Britain, it is true, withdrew from Burma almost simultaneously with its departure from India, and months earlier it had been clear that it was preparing to do so. America also had given full independence to the Philippines, fulfilling a timetable begun before the war started. But at the time when the curtain lifts on this phase in Asia – the middle of 1947 – it was still uncertain whether the Dutch and French were to leave Indonesia and Indo-China. Each was engaged in a military struggle with nationalist movements; each was trying to organize local governments, rather less extreme than the intransigent nationalists, which would fight the extremists and would permit some place in government for the former colonial overlords.

In 1947 these struggles did not endanger world peace. In the immediate aftermath of the war South-east Asia enjoyed a certain isolation. New and independent India was too much occupied with domestic affairs to assert itself in the region. China was in disorder, Japan in ruins. Britain and America had systematically withdrawn their power. But it did not need a very long sight to realize that these conditions were exceptional and would not last. When formidable land powers were once again consolidated in

Asia, the significance of South-east Asia as the Balkans of the continent would inevitably appear. A group of small countries on the edge of great empires gives rise to every kind of competition in power politics.

6 CENTRAL ASIA

THE fifth of the 'natural' divisions of the Asian continent is Central Asia. It is a vast territory, containing the huge expanse of Turkestan and Tibet. It is the most barely inhabited part of the great land-mass but with a strange variety of people, many of them nomadic. It is peculiar because most of it belongs to the Russian Empire and has not taken part in the experience of emancipation and new birth of the rest of Asia.

The majority of the inhabitants of Turkestan belong to different sections of the Turkic peoples, who developed one of the distinctive branches of Islamic civilization.* Bukhara and Samarkand are famous cities of Moslem culture. From early in the nineteenth century an increasingly large part of the Turkic population passed under the political control of a Western country, Russia. In many respects Russia both before and after the Bolshevik revolution exercised an influence different from that of other Western powers. The part of Central Asia which was subdued by Russia became Westernized – but it was Westernization of a different pattern from that elsewhere in Asia.

Russia's advance into Asia was imperialist. But its imperialism differed from that of the West European countries because Russia's expansion was by land and not, like that of the other Western countries, by sea. No natural boundaries divided Russia from Asia, and geographically, if not culturally, Russia is an Asian country. Thus when the Russians occupied a territory they did not, like the maritime Westerners, merely impose upon it an upper caste of administrators or traders who could be fairly easily thrown off when the indigenous forces reasserted themselves. In-

* The Tadjiks are the exception. They speak Persian.

stead, Russia organized and assimilated the territory; in the long run it became bone of Russia's bone; its ethnographical composition was often changed; a large Russian population moved in and intermarried with the local people; emancipation was almost unthinkable.

Russia's empire in Central Asia was divided into two parts. One part, such as the Kazakh steppes, was a more or less empty land suitable for colonization by Russians.* This the Russians administered directly as an integral part of Russia. On the other hand, the Khanates of Central Asia were ancient political entities, even if rather chaotic ones. Here the Russians, in the stage of their expansion before the Bolshevik revolution, did no more than establish political supremacy. The Khanates – Khiva and Bukhara – were reduced to protectorates, but preserved, and Russia controlled them by means of the ancient machinery.†

It has sometimes been suggested that Russia in these transactions was less of an aggressor against Asia than the maritime Western powers. Certainly the Russians were less colour conscious; they intermarried and they never asserted racial superiority over the peoples of Asia, and this may have saved them from some ill-feeling. There was only one serious revolt against the government – in 1898 – and that was short-lived. Yet this does not alter the fact that Russia, like the Western powers, had been a battering ram against the existing order in Asia.

Throughtout the nineteenth century and early years of the twentieth the Russian advance continued. The impulse behind Russia was described not unfairly by the Tsarist Chancellor, Prince Gorchakov, in a note which he sent to all the interested powers in 1864:

'The position of Russia in Central Asia is that of all civilized states which come into contact with half-savage wandering tribes possessing no fixed social organization. It invariably happens in such cases that the interests of security on the frontier, and of commercial relations, compel the more civilized state to exercise

---

* The same was true of Siberia, in the north of the continent, which Russia had occupied by the middle of the nineteenth century.

† One Khanate – Kokand – was abolished and treated as a province of Russia.

a certain ascendancy over neighbours whose turbulence and nomad existence render them difficult to live with.'

At one time Russia seemed likely to go further than this. Because the Chinese government was weakening, it was tempted to penetrate into the Chinese Empire and it threatened both Sinkiang and Manchuria. But this generated a reaction; Japan feared Russian supremacy and took over the role of defending Manchuria which China should have discharged. The result was the Russo-Japanese war of 1905, Russia's defeat, and the temporary check to the Tsars.

As Russia rolled slowly forward it had caused alarm also to the Western imperialist powers in South Asia, especially to the British in India. They thought they saw the beginning of an Anglo-Russian combat for supremacy in Asia. But the century passed without open war. Distances between the bases of the Russian and British armies were so immense, the means of transport still so limited, that each country had room to hit about it without actually coming into conflict. Central Asia was a kind of giant cotton wool, absorbing and muffling blows.

As long as Tsarist rule continued in Russia the effects in Central Asia were still mild, extremely so in those parts where the Khanates had been preserved, but also in the areas directly ruled.* The Russians were far less positive than the British in India; they built no schools or universities and fostered no middle-class civilization. The radical changes were to begin only with the Bolshevik revolution. The first step then was the abolition of the Khanates. Religion was dethroned. Islam, like Christianity, had to take its chance of survival in a society officially atheist.

In 1925 Soviet Central Asia was reorganized politically into the five republics of Uzbekistan, Tadzhikistan, Kirghizistan, Turkmenia, and Kazakhstan. Nominally they were constituent republics of the U.S.S.R., though the achievement by some of them of this status was delayed until 1936. They were supposed to correspond to the ethnic groups among the Turkic peoples. In fact the dis-

---

* The Khans were given a great deal of liberty. No Russian Resident was present continuously at their capitals. The Khans neglected even to extirpate slavery, though they had bound themselves to do so.

tinction between most of these peoples is slight, and it would have been quite proper, on ethnic grounds, to have formed a single republic of Turkestan. But Russian policy was evidently to divide Turkestan into a number of units in order to prevent the rise of a Turkic nationalist movement which might have challenged Russian control. Moscow opposed the movements in the different republics to collaborate closely with one another.

Though in theory the republics enjoyed a measure of sovereignty, in fact they were more closely controlled by Moscow than the Khanates had been in the past. At first Moscow treated them indulgently and no such sweeping changes took place in Central Asian society as had happened in Russia. Though the chiefs and the very wealthy had been eliminated, the economic and much of the social system continued as it had been before the revolution. But in 1929 a radical transformation began. The Russian government included Central Asia in the collectivization of agriculture. By this means the old tribal system was finally shattered and the hold of the former landlords broken. Still more radical in its effects was the nationalization of the herds of the nomads. The nomad people were rounded up like prisoners of war; there was a huge mortality of cattle; thousands of the tribesmen escaped into Chinese Turkestan, and others were deported into different parts of the Russian Empire. In all the republics the Russian government began an intensive programme to modernize, to develop industry, to foster the growth of towns, and to train and educate a new class of leaders and technicians by whom this transformation might be effected.

While maintaining its absolute political authority, the Russian government tried in the years before the war to assuage nationalist resentment by giving an ostentatious encouragement to local languages, literature, folk-songs, music, and art. This was the liberal 'nationalities' policy which was much extolled. It had certainly some success in winning a grateful attachment; but the feeling of the Turkic peoples was shown during the war with Hitler, when they proved one of the least reliable parts of the Russian army.

It happened thus that the experience of the Asian peoples of Central Asia in their contact with the West proved in many ways different from that of the people of the rest of Asia. It is true that, like the Indians, the Turkic peoples had been subjected to a Western power. But instead of reacting by means of a fierce nationalist movement, by which their independence could be regained, they were swamped and swallowed by the Western power. By accident or design, Russia had foiled Asian nationalism more effectively than any of the other Western countries. The Turkic peoples have not 'stood up'. They have not been unbound.

Like the other peoples of Asia, the Turkic peoples became Westernized, but the Western attitudes and ideas which they accepted were different from those which made up the civilization of the Europeanized intelligentsia of the rest of the Asian continent. Instead of the humanism which the Indians or Burmese derived from Britain the Turkic peoples were presented with technical education; instead of a sceptical rationalism, with Marxist dogma; instead of democratic ideas, with the assumption that the best form of government was Communist Party dictatorship. Parliament, the rule of law, constitutionalism, the beauties of compromise – all the essential ideas of Western civilization in India – meant nothing at all in Turkestan, at least after the Communist revolution. But in its place was the worship of technical knowledge and the factory and the ardent belief that the supreme interest of man was to build industrial civilization.

The peoples of Central Asia in the parts which lay outside the borders of the U.S.S.R. did not undergo this peculiar Russian variant of Westernization. In fact they remained less Westernized than almost any other part of the Asian continent. They were citizens of the periphery of the Chinese Empire, and while that Empire was decaying they remained in a backwater. For many years the great province of Sinkiang passed out of the control of the central government of China and was in the hands of a warlord whose least interest was in promoting social change or in breathing into the province the new ideas from outside. His authority was constantly threatened by the Turkic tribesmen – and by Chinese Moslems – and he maintained himself partly through aid given him by the Russians. The Russians exacted a price, but their interest was the strategic control of the area; they did not seek to turn upon it the same revolutionary influences which had reshaped their own Asian territory. At the end of the war between China and Japan, Chiang Kai-shek managed, rather surprisingly, to reassert the central government's authority in Sinkiang, and Russia acquiesced. But even then the peoples of Chinese Turkestan did not enter upon a period of any drastic change.

The most interesting part of Central Asia, Tibet, seemed in 1947 to stand even further apart from radical change. For centuries Tibet had been a theocracy, a federation of Lamaist monasteries, its system of government being one of the curiosities of the modern world. Until the beginning of this century it admitted the general supervision of China, which was usually exercised laxly and indulgently. After the fall of the Manchu Empire the head of the theocracy, the Dalai Lama, established virtual independence, and in doing this received the sympathy of the British government in India. The British interest was that Tibet should be a buffer state; if no other power controlled it, Britain had no desire to undertake the control itself. Thus Tibet was permitted to remain a sealed land, untouched by the outside world. But the changes in the rest of Asia which had come about were soon to cause commotion even in this unchanging country. For Tibet, 1947 was the prelude not to liberation but to subjection.

7   THE EXTERNAL POWERS

IN this picture of Asia in 1947, round the ring on the outside, loom the non-Asian great powers—nor are they so very much on the outside. In the previous century and a half they, and not the Asian countries, had had the main say about what was to happen in Asia. It would take time for the world to change the habit of expecting them to do so again and for the Asian countries to cease to let their attitudes be affected by what had happened in the past.

In 1947 three of these countries, Britain, America, and Russia, were of predominant influence. France, Holland, and Portugal, though with illustrious histories of adventure in Asia, had ceased to shape the drama on the great stage of Asia, and were in course of being compelled by circumstances to recognize that it was useless to try to do so.

The interests and policies of the three major external powers have already been described implicitly in the picture of the Asian countries.

Britain was anxious to retire from the scene. It had been more deeply involved in Asia than the other two. For more than a century it had performed the astonishing feat of sustaining the Indian Empire with a force of fewer than 2,000 British civil servants and less than 60,000 British troops. It had been the arch empire-maker among the Western powers. It had written into history a record of which, on balance, it need not be ashamed. The creation of the British Raj had been a romantic adventure. But the British people in the post-war mood of 1945 decided that it was time the adventure ended.

During the twenties and thirties British opinion about Empires had firmly changed. By the end of the war they were considered morally wrong and economically unsound, and this by all manner of people who had formerly applauded them. People in Britain had been shocked at seeing how little support was given to British arms during the war by Malayans and Burmese when their countries were attacked by Japan, and they drew the conclusion that British imperialism was more deeply disliked than they had realized. But the prime cause of the resolve in Britain to lay down responsibility was an understanding of the strength of Oriental nationalism. This was seen to be one of the elemental forces of the age, likely to increase in vigour rather than diminish. With prudent instinct, the British people was determined not to come into collision with it.

The assessment of the realities of the new age, this resolution to come to terms with Indian nationalism and not to fight it, had really been made in the thirties, when Gandhi had confronted the British government with the alternative either of governing with unremitting coercion or else of transferring its power. But in the thirties there was still time for manoeuvre; withdrawal could be by degrees. War speeded up the process.*

* The dominant aim of British government in India in the first two post-war years was to prevent a clash between Indian nationalism and the British

With the surrender made in India – and also in Pakistan, Burma, and Ceylon – popular sentiment in Britain was at first in favour of writing off its interest in Asia. These were the years of peril at home – economic peril from the dollar crisis, military peril from the advance of Russia in Europe. They were years of preoccupation with the peaceful social revolution in Britain. Probably at this time a majority of the electorate in Britain would have been indifferent if it had been told that it need never again concern itself about Asian affairs. It was happy to see old ideas about Britain's vital interests in the East go by the board.

The British Labour Government, it is true, was less irresponsible. At the time that it was transferring political power it was already proposing the economic aid which, at heavy cost, it would offer the governments of free Asia in an endeavour to assist their first years. But the new birth of British interest in Asia which was to follow from this effort still lay in the future.

If Britain was giving up its position in India, it was obviously in no condition to exert influence in these years in the Far East. Cheerfully it left China and Japan as an American sphere of influence; 1947 found Britain virtually without a China policy.

America in these years was as anxious to take positive steps in Asia as Britain was to be retiring. To-day an effort is needed if American sentiment at that time is to be properly recollected, so different was it from the sentiment to-day. The American attitude was then, as it always must be, complex, since it is made up of the struggles of a great many conflicting instincts and emotions. Strong forces still made for the isolationism which had been the predominant attitude in the previous two decades. Yet on the whole Americans had come to believe that their country, by virtue of its power being so suddenly increased in relation to the rest of the world, must take increased responsibility in organizing a

power still in India. As long as Britain had the responsibility for maintaining law and order, there was the danger that this clash would occur, however resolved the British government was upon extricating itself eventually from India. The tremendous tension between Hindus and Moslems caused repeated massacres all the way across northern India. It seemed likely that British forces might have to be called on in order to stop the killing. In doing so they might collide almost inadvertently with the forces of nationalism.

peaceful world. Their own security demanded that they should pursue more adventurous policies than in the past. This combined with a new stirring of interest in the outside world, which appeared more fascinating than it had used to do. Asia especially attracted Americans, for while the complexities of Europe baffled them and left them hopeless they saw in the Asian countries a new romance.

By long tradition Americans dislike empires. Their schools, their celebrations on every July 4th, their incantations convince them that the beginning of their own greatness was the disruption of Britain's empire in America. Their sympathies were stirred by the Asian peoples who had been subjected by European empires. If they had been unable to give them active assistance in procuring their liberation, they would at least applaud the act when it was done. By its own liberal policy towards the Philippines, America was able to claim that it practised what it preached. The emancipation of India, Burma, Indonesia, and the other Asian nations seemed to America the start of an auspicious new age, requiring America's benevolence. American missionaries, business men, and educators made themselves available to the lands beginning their new existence.

To the cynical eye, some of the American conceptions at the time might seem curious. America saw modern Oriental history as an exciting spectacle, whose theme was the formation of new Asian nations. They thought of these nations as young and fresh; their great past did not interest them very much. It was taken for granted that what had been wrong with these countries was their subjection to foreign rule: once they had been emancipated, all would be plain sailing. Almost nobody wondered aloud whether they might not start quarrelling among themselves. It was assumed that it was the destiny of the liberated countries to become constitutional democracies, and also that it would be their desire to equate their social life more and more with that of America.

At this stage many of the Asian countries felt a reciprocal cordiality for this great well-wisher. In a formidable world, was it not an excellent thing to have a mighty and disinterested friend, which had never been guilty of imperialism, except on a small scale and more or less accidentally in the Philippines? How far away was 1947 from 1955. At that time America signified the Western country which had never had an Empire, at least of any reprehensible size. It meant the country of Washington and Jefferson, the apostle of the independence of nations, the anti-imperialist.

It is true that one shadow hung over the mutual sympathy. America had dropped the atom bomb upon Japan; the bomb had not been used against Germany. Already the Asian Communists were fanning the feeling of race hatred which might grow out of this. But America's culpability appeared to Asians less then than it does to-day.

If America's good will was offered to all Asia, its practical interests at the time were concentrated on China. America's historic connexion in Asia was with China, as Britain's had been with India. Trade connexions had been reinforced by interest in missionary and educational enterprises. Few towns in America were without residents who had worked in China. During the closing years of the war, as America planned its future actions, it was natural to suppose that the hard core of the post-war organization of Asia should be collaboration between America and China. After the defeat of Japan, the Kuomintang Government would be the most genuinely nationalist and potentially strong authority in Asia; in the eyes of Washington the government of Chiang Kai-shek appeared in 1947 a far more substantial thing than the new and still untested government of Congress India.

Hence the American efforts – which were all to fail – to buttress the Kuomintang. Hence the efforts to overcome the disorders in China by bringing about the coalition of Kuomintang and Communists – efforts which were also to fail. Hence too the ever greater involvement of America in Far Eastern affairs.

Russia, the third of the external powers, had by contrast appeared, up to 1947, less involved than might have been expected. The world had supposed that it would steep itself in Asian politics; ever since the Bolshevik revolution, it had seemed that the Asian continent might be the best target for Communist propaganda, and that fires started there might engulf the world. At various times before the war, Moscow's interest in Asia had made the Western world tremble. But in the war and immediate post-war period, Stalin's government seemed, to the relief of onlookers, to be foregoing some of its opportunities. At first Moscow conducted a policy which was more in the interests of the Russian state than of international communism. At the Yalta conference it insisted on the recreation for Russia of the privileged position which it had enjoyed in Manchuria before the Russo-Japanese war; after it came into the war and occupied Manchuria, it stole and transported to Russia the equipment of the factories which had been built by the Japanese, and which the Chinese had coveted as the spoils of war. Both acts were hardly likely to commend Russia, or the communism which Russia patronized, to Chinese nationalism.

The truth seems to be that Stalin and his advisers disbelieved in the likelihood of the Chinese Communists overthrowing the Kuomintang and becoming the government of the country. They thought that at best the Chinese Communists could maintain themselves in authority in a backwoods part of the country. Why should Moscow complicate its relations with the Kuomintang by backing what seemed to be a hopeless cause? The Kuomintang government was evidently by no means antipathetic to Russia. Moscow found its interests served by a weak Chinese government which would need to look to it for favour. Chiang Kai-shek might be deferential to Moscow because he needed a counterweight to too much benevolence from America. All things considered, the Kuomintang suited Moscow rather well.

Even if Stalin had been better informed about the prospects and strength of the Chinese Communists, it is not certain that he would have been more energetic in backing them. Every dictator of Russia is two personalities, the Pope of international Communism, and the head of the Russian government. Can Russia ever feel entirely easy at the existence of a huge military power in China, even if it is a Communist power? China's interests as a state do not necessarily coincide with Russia's. Russia is a Western power. Will a strong China always acquiesce in Russia occupying so large a part of Central Asia? It was inevitable that once a Chinese Communist Government was installed, Russia must applaud it and stand by its side. But Russia did not have to hasten the day.

Thus in 1947 Russia's zeal for Communism in China was tepid. But events were soon to move beyond Moscow's control.

8 ASIA'S GREAT MEN

In this panorama of Asia in 1947, who at that time were the typical leaders? One outshone all the others. This was Gandhi. But Gandhi was to be assassinated within a few months; he was an exceptional figure, unhappily not able to make general and normal his very peculiar modes of political behaviour. Since 1947 the light which he shed upon Asia has slowly waned.

In 1947 he was, however, still the supreme personality of Asia. In most Asian countries, however far away from India, the young men, if asked to name the figure who spoke for them, would at that time have named Gandhi. What, then, were his qualities?

The strange fact is that Gandhi, though by outward signs very much a traditional Indian, derived many of his ideas and also his attitudes from the West. To Indians who looked behind the appearances, he seemed a very untraditional figure. Though he was accepted as a religious teacher, he devoted most of his life to politics; none of the major prophets of Hinduism had ever done the same. He regarded society, as it existed in all countries, as steeped in corruption, but instead of withdrawing altogether from its taint, which was the traditional response of the Hindu holy man, he was an enthusiast for creating new model societies, based on simple moral principles and so small and self-contained as to be controllable. From his early days in South Africa he was experimenting with these Utopias. If, later, he abandoned the attempt, it was because he was distracted by national politics in India. The passion for Utopias links him with the English and American philanthropists of the nineteenth century who were haunted by the same interests. Some of his other interests came from the Victorian radicals and Nonconformists of England, and were not native to India. Individualism, iconoclasm, the cult of austerity, the emphasis on self-discipline – these were of course not unknown to India, but in Gandhi they took the form common to English puritanism. Though in theory he dedicated all secular activities to the glory of God, and worked as God's instrument, it seems unlikely that he enjoyed any mystical experiences of union with deity such as have been described by nearly all the great Hindu religious leaders. His relation to God was more like that of the devout Protestant whose religion it is to live a strenuous life devoted to good works.*

This was the man who in 1947 enjoyed the prestige of being the principal agent in shaking down the mighty British Raj, and who for two generations had been the main director of the force of Indian nationalism. Probably this nationalism would in any case have overthrown the Raj. But Gandhi, by his political genius, enabled it to do so with a minimum of bloodshed, and therefore without causing lasting hostility between India and the West, and without provoking further convulsions in Indian society. That the dissolution of the Raj came about so peacefully was one of the miracles of our time. It was one of the instances of one man's influence causing history to take one course when, given other personal influences, it might as easily have taken another.

The achievement of Gandhi was to associate nationalism with the admirable and pacific ethical concepts summed up in the term Gandhism. While he lived, ardent nationalists in Asia could believe in pacifism, in the value of the individual soul, and in his other humane ideas. There was of course no essential connexion between them. Already in 1947 the danger was that with Gandhi's removal the humanity would also disappear from Asian nationalism.

The danger was the more obvious because in 1947 there were already a number of other notable leaders of Asian nationalism,

* The purely Indian element in Gandhi should of course not be underrated. It was a Jain element rather than a Hindu one. His doctrine of nonviolence came probably from the extreme respect for life of the Jains. His method of gaining his way by spectacular fasts, and the organization of life in his ashram, were drawn from Indian tradition. His rather ambiguous attitude to caste — condemnation combined with a longing belief that an ideally organized caste system might be desirable — could have been found only in an Indian.

and none was a propagandist of the special type of ethical ideas which appealed so strongly to Gandhi. Even among the Hindus there were national leaders who owed their strength to standing for stark nationalism with all the moderating and ethical elements of Gandhism shorn away. Such had been Subhas Chandra Bose, the dissident Congress leader who had fought Gandhi in 1939 for the control of Congress and had been outwitted; during the war he had fled from India to join the Axis powers and had organized the so-called Indian National Army out of the prisoners taken by the Japanese. Bose died at the end of the war. If he had survived, he would have been a dangerous enemy to Gandhism. So were the leaders of the Hindu Mahasabha, a Hindu party outside Congress which was devoted to nationalism pure and simple. None of its leaders won more than local fame. But it was a powerful movement. A sympathizer with the party was to assassinate Gandhi in 1948.

The main leaders of Asian nationalism outside India in 1947 were Jinnah in Pakistan, Sukarno in Indonesia, Aung San in Burma, and Chiang Kai-shek in China. All had certain similarities. Jinnah was a man of inflexible will. He was worldly, if austere. He had a perfect sense of political timing, and a correct intuition about the strength of the various political forces. The Moslems of the Indian sub-continent saw in him the perfect expression of their aspiration; hence his authority.

In Burma, Aung San expressed similarly the resolution of young Burmans to be free of British rule. Of all the national leaders he was perhaps the boldest and most adroit. Before the war he had fled to Japan. During the Japanese invasion of Burma he organized a Burmese force to assist them; then, because Japan did not satisfy the demands of Burmese nationalism, switched sides and supported, on conditions which may not have been very clear, the returning British. In 1946 he became the head of a national cabinet to which the British would transfer power. Before the process was completed he was murdered, together with half his cabinet, by a rival nationalist of the older generation. Because he championed nationalism so ruthlessly, was such a forceful personality, and came to such a dramatic end, he had been canonized in Burmese memory. Yet nobody can pretend that he brought spiritual light. He was a secular leader such as Asia had seen upon innumerable occasions.*

President Sukarno, of Indonesia, was a rather similar figure, though less ruthless and more eloquent. He was the golden voice of the Indonesian revolution, and for this reason embodied Indonesian nationalism.

Chiang Kai-shek, of China, was in personality the most notable of the non-Gandhian leaders of 1947. He was a Christian convert, belonging to the Southern Methodists; nevertheless he was attracted by Confucian ideas, since he considered these good for discipline, and tried to promote a Confucian revival. He was in no sense a liberator of the human mind, the inspirer of new ideals of universal philanthropy, or even the champion of any coherent body of new doctrine. Like Jinnah, he was a man of inflexible will, and like other nationalists he gave the appearance of pursuing the national interests to the exclusion of all other considerations. For some years he had the gift of making himself the symbol of the hopes of Chinese nationalism, and of its determination to survive the attacks by Japan. To this he owed his position and prestige, which he could never have gained merely by his skill in playing off factions within the Kuomintang, formidable though this was.†

These leaders were all men of powerful personality, whether in will or emotion or instinctive knowledge of when to act. But they had all made their figure in the world – even Gandhi – because they happened to express just the ideas or attitudes for which people were waiting. Without this, most of them, whatever their talent, would have died little known. Thus the history of Asia is genuinely the history of the people or at least of the awakened classes. The leaders seemed to express exactly what most of their educated fellow-countrymen would have desired to say, but could not by themselves utter.

In 1947 the intelligentsia, whose opinion was so decisive in preserving or killing a political régime, was at a critical moment.

* His successor, U Nu, was of the Gandhian type. But Aung San remains a portent.

† Syngman Rhee was of a rather similar type. But in 1947 he had not yet become world-famous.

Nationalism, to which it had devoted itself with complete fervour, was about to triumph, and Asia to be free. What would happen afterwards when Asia moved towards the phase of reorganizing society by its own volition? No single interest or passion would then unite the intelligentsia. The tasks were obvious – to industrialize, to begin the painful task of converting nations of peasants into nations of factory workers, to organize social services, to develop administrative efficiency, to end confusion, to bring more ordered purpose to society, to enable the peoples of the East to live on terms more approaching economic equality with the West. But by what political means could this best be done?

The probability seemed to be that the influence of the intelligentsia would continue to be as decisive in the next decade as it had been before 1947. But first the intelligentsia would have to clarify its own ideas and aims. Thus a new struggle was to take place in its soul – the struggle between the different ideologies which competed as offering the best hope for the new age in Asia.

All the subsequent great events in Asia – the transformation of China, the parliamentary politics of India, war in Korea – have reflected the conflicts in the mind of the thinking part of Asia. The student in the bookshop is in the long run more important than the leaders of the parties. Upon him beats all the propaganda of all opposed sides and forces. He makes the choices, by processes which may be very obscure, which determine the next course in Asian history.

The opportunity to make a choice is one of the peculiar features in Asian history to-day. It lays a burden on this generation. In the past the child born into an Oriental society found himself in a vast organization in which his duties and proper attitudes were prescribed, his rights to some extent guaranteed and his rewards, material and psychological, assured, provided he did what was expected of him. He was carried along in the great caravan of society, and if there was suffering to be endured on the way there were plenty to share it. Life was not lonely or puzzling. But after the social changes of the present day the map of the world and society which was formerly given at birth to each newcomer has been torn up. This generation must decide for itself which way to go.

PART TWO *The Chinese Revolution*

SINCE 1947 *the scene in Asia has changed. The decisive, sombre event which transformed the prospects was the victory of Communism in China. The revolution in China, which at one time seemed to have petered out in the military government of Chiang Kai-shek, came once again monstrously to life. China became, first Communist, second a great power.*

'Let China sleep,' said Napoleon. 'When it wakes, the world will be sorry.' Our generation has experienced the awakening.

The Chinese revolution has been called the 'undoubted culminating event of Asian resurgence'. It was certainly this. By its intense nationalism and defiance of the West it has advertised the fact. But it is more besides. It is a Communist revolution which has sought to transform China from top to bottom, and to create a pattern of society which, though Asian and growing out of China's past and by no means a mere copy of Russia, is something new in Asia's experience. This has had effects far beyond China's borders. It has made it at least possible that the 'standing up' of the rest of Asia will result, not in a continuation and development of the liberal civilization such as has been evolving in India, but in the eclipse of the civilization by Communism.

Nationalism and the desire for independence from the West were the prime forces almost everywhere in Asia before the Chinese Communist victory. After the Chinese revolution the possibility exists that these forces in all the other countries of Asia may become associated with Communism. By all political means and by propaganda, China is bidding for their support. Also since China by its revolution has become a great military power, with centralized authority and with rejuvenated vigour, the danger has grown up that

China may expand beyond its borders, and spread Communism over the adjacent countries by force or political manoeuvres.

The new system in China is thus the crucial matter for study in Asia to-day. Its origin, and a portrait of the civilization as it exists at the moment, are the subject of this part of the book.

9   THE POST-WAR KUOMINTANG

In the summer of 1947 the Kuomintang and the Chinese Communists faced each other, getting ready for the final struggle.

What were the chances of both sides as they prepared for the final battles?

The Kuomintang had still great advantages. It was internationally recognized as the only government of China. It had survived the attack by Japan. Through war-time propaganda by its Western allies, Chiang Kai-shek had been built up in the minds of many people in Europe and America as one of the great figures of the world; he was represented as an austere warrior saint, incorruptible even if his colleagues were not. In China also he still appeared to large sections of the country as the figure of by far the greatest dimensions. Huge armies were under his command, numbering in all nearly three million men; a part had been equipped by America and trained by American instructors; and Chiang could count, if all went well, on more substantial aid from America in future. He held the railways. He held the ports. He could raise revenues. He held all the best strategic positions.

But there was a debit side to the account. The government over which Chiang Kai-shek presided had deteriorated since the start of the war with Japan. For seven years it had sustained the national cause – at times falteringly and not very gloriously but in substance unyielding – and at the end it broke under too much strain. The war had worn out the Kuomintang. It was the war's principal victim. When the war ended, and the government returned from its remote war-time centre in Chungking to the wealthy coastal regions, the degeneration became suddenly plain.

From almost the highest leaders of the Kuomintang down to the lowest functionary, one interest gripped them all – to recoup themselves for the sufferings of the war years. Seldom can an administration have been so little troubled about appearances. The various reconstruction projects which were financed by CINNRA – the Chinese equivalent of UNRRA in Europe – gave them opportunity. Stories of corruption may have been exaggerated, but those which were true were often so staggering as almost to excite disbelief.*

A party and government which was seized with this obsession of corruption could give no constructive lead to the nation. It ceased to stand for any ideas. At all times, ideas had been the weak side of the Kuomintang. Certainly it had an ideology of a kind. Officially it was based on Sun Yat-sen's three principles – nationalism, democracy and welfare. But these principles were vague, and the post-war practice of the Kuomintang rendered them a mockery. The more idealist members of the Kuomintang either retired into private life or withdrew into sullen and ineffective opposition: a few switched sides altogether and joined the Communists. The only faction in the party which was attached seriously to ideas was one which wanted a return to the old-fashioned Confucian ideas which Chinese progressives had until then believed to be the greatest impediment to true enlightenment.

* There had been a foretaste of what was to come in the war-time scandals of the traffic on the Burma road, which was China's main life line. The road should have been used for bringing in essential supplies, but was to a startling extent used by ministers and officials for bringing in luxury goods which they sold on the black market. The opium traffic had always been a sinister institution in Kuomintang China, and its poison ramified through society. It was maintained as a deliberate act of state policy in order to raise revenue for the army. But though some of the darker practices of the Kuomintang go back well beyond the final years of collapse, it should not be overlooked that a terrible deterioration did take place. Before the war with Japan the Kuomintang had been a genuinely creative force, full of vigour even if incompetent. It had some notable constructive achievements to its credit. Among these were the building of a great network of motor roads, the rapid extension of cotton planting, the development of rural health services, some large hydraulic works, and the organization of a modern banking system. For a very short while the currency was actually stabilized.

Bankrupt in ideas and spiritual force, the Kuomintang had to seek other means to maintain its authority. It found these especially in the secret police. To organize a secret police comes easily to the Chinese, because for centuries one of the most flourishing elements in their society has been secret societies. It was simple for the government to recruit some of these in its service. During the latter part of the history of the Kuomintang, there existed five or six separate secret police forces, each of them attached to different leaders or factions in the party. The most formidable was controlled by a sinister commander named Tai Li, who was one of the main pillars of support of Chiang Kai-shek. The agents of the secret police were thought to be everywhere, and fear spread throughout the country. There was special resentment at the interest of the police in spying upon the students, who had always regarded themselves as a privileged class in China. Because of the police network, there existed a large number of political prisoners, though just how many was never known. Certainly the number was never anything like that in totalitarian countries such as Nazi Germany or Russia. Besides making arrests, the secret organizations carried out assassinations of those whom the Kuomintang regarded as dangerous enemies. The number of these may not have been very large but they excited the fiercest anger. The murder of a revered professor at Yunnan university caused special fury. This terror organized by the police was enough to inspire the maximum desire for revenge by the opposition, not enough to paralyse it.

Another cause of the alienation of the influential public from the government was the collapse of the currency, which may have been due in part to the difficulties of the war and post-war circumstances, but which was also caused by the corruption, cynicism and inefficiency of administration. The Chinese dollar fell to depths never before explored by a currency: its descent was as interminable and profound as that of the bad angels. An uncontrollable inflation generates within society a war of all against all, a terrible sense of insecurity, and a longing for the hand of authority. 'If you wish to make a revolution,' said Lenin, 'debauch the currency.' The debauched Chinese dollar dug the grave of the Kuomintang.

In spite of all these defects of the party, were not its immense armies a force sufficiently strong to counteract them and keep it in power? Unhappily for the Kuomintang, the general rot had spread to the soldiers also. Most regiments were irregularly paid, and the arrangements for commissariat and medical service were scandalous; in many regiments the pay was made by the government to the commanding officer, who was left to pay his officers, who were then left to pay their men; most of the money never reached the ranks. In consequence soldiers had little will to fight.*

The condition of the Kuomintang in 1947 was thus precarious – a party divided into a number of cliques led by politicians, most of them ageing, who had ceased to be interested in any particular programme, and whose main function was to provide for their adherents. Over them Chiang Kai-shek presided, owing his position partly to his skill in playing off one faction against another. It was not to be wondered at if patriotic Chinese – the Chinese who wanted progress, strong government, and the restoration of China's progress – turned away in despair from the Kuomintang. According to traditional Chinese philosophy, a government was legitimate only so long as it had a 'mandate from Heaven'; the existence of the mandate was proved by its success. In 1947 the general view was that the Kuomintang had lost the mandate.

The revolution which had begun in 1911 had petered out before its tasks were accomplished because the Kuomintang, once the agent of revolution, had lost its revolutionary force. It had no programme and shrank away from every project of social reform. If the revolution was to be completed, the nation would have to seek for another agent which would take up the work left only half done by the Kuomintang.

The politically conscious classes, which were not committed to the Kuomintang or who had broken with it – professors and students, some business men, leaders of splinter groups which had broken from the Kuomintang, dissatisfied generals – began to wonder whether the future did not lie with the one great organized counter-force, the Communists.

* Some colonels were very anxious to get their men killed. They then drew their pay. Regimental rolls showed large numbers of men who had long ceased to exist.

At this stage relatively little was still known about the Communists. Some of the few facts which were certain were romantic and excited interest. For twenty years they had successfully defied the Kuomintang. They controlled very formidable armies. Many foreigners who were not Communists spoke of them with more respect than they spoke of the Kuomintang. They were said to be spectacularly non-corrupt. And they were disciplined. Sun Yat-sen used to say that the special malady of the Chinese people was that they were more than naturally undisciplined. They were like a tray of sand: if the tray was shaken, the grains dispersed in all directions; there was no cohesive principle. The Communists appeared to be the first in modern China who had invented effective discipline. If it was maintained by terror, that did not deter those who in Kuomintang China were more impressed by the evils apparent all around them from indiscipline than by its excesses.

The Communists had, moreover, a doctrine and philosophy. It was a movement devoted to an idea. 'The revolution is a doctrine armed' said Burke of the first French revolution; the same was true of the Chinese Communist revolution. The doctrine was Marxism and Leninism. In fact these were interpreted with a bold disregard where theory did not fit in with practice. Thus in China the Communists came to power chiefly by means of a peasant revolt, while according to Marxism a Communist revolution should have been brought about by the urban working classes; this was simply ignored. But all the elements of theory which fitted in with the circumstances of China – the doctrines of class war, of increasing misery of the oppressed, of the materialist interpretation of history – were proclaimed by a very efficient propaganda machine. Chinese were encouraged to think that Communist revolution was inevitable in history and that those who fought against it were resisting what had already been determined.

The dark sides to the record of the Communists were, of course, known. In the early thirties, when they had organized a government in the rural areas of Kiangsi and Fukien, they had practised terror against the rural gentry and merchants. There had been horrifying killings. But after the Long March and the move to the north-west it was said that their ferocity had abated; they had tried to conciliate or reassure some of the smaller landlords. It is true that stories continued to circulate of atrocities in some areas – of the poorer people being organized to lynch wealthier inhabitants – but the tendency was to discount many of these stories as Kuomintang propaganda.

Because the Communists based their hopes on peasant armies and guerilla war, all their successes up to this time had been in the villages and country districts. They controlled no city until the post-war period. Therefore nobody knew how they would administer urban society or whether the party, exposed to the temptations of the great centres of commerce, would remain uncorrupt. But this did not rule them out from being allowed to make the experiment of turning China into a Communist republic.

For much of China in 1947 Communism signified two things, a manifest vigour and a new hope rising in a country which saw nothing else in which to put any hope at all. For this reason, as the two sides got ready for the final combat, a considerable part of the social classes whose interests were most likely to suffer from Communism felt in spite of themselves a sympathy for the Communists. News of Communist victories might bring anxiety, but also a sense of awareness that great historic events were happening which it would be useless to regard merely as distasteful.

IO   THE KUOMINTANG FALLS

The end, or near end, of the long struggle between the Communists and the Kuomintang came within less than two years of the heavy fighting being resumed.

For the previous ten years, right through the period of the war with Japan, there had been a stalemate between the Kuomintang and the Communists. Though the Communists held very large rural areas they were not strong enough to storm the towns. On the other hand, the Kuomintang could not reoccupy the lost rural areas or bring to pitched battle the Communist guerilla armies.

But since the end of the war changes had come about. The credit of the Kuomintang with the public had declined steeply. The Communists had acquired modern weapons, part being the stocks transferred to them by Russia after the Japanese army in Manchuria had surrendered.

Chiang Kai-shek's armies broke in his hand. He ordered them forward to attack the Communists in Manchuria. They were defeated, were besieged in the towns and surrendered. Chiang was faulty in his generalship in allowing so much of his army to perish uselessly.

South of the Great Wall the events repeated themselves. The Communists were now for the first time able to overwhelm garrisons in the cities, and one by one the great towns fell. The railways were cut. The Kuomintang could no longer pretend that the Communists were no more than insurgents.

Why should the Kuomintang soldiers fight seriously? Before 1947 there had been the belief that the Kuomintang had a future; but afterwards there grew up a general belief that it was doomed. Nobody will fight for a régime which Heaven is felt to have abandoned. The Communists, exploiting the trading instincts of the Chinese people, used against Chiang a very successful device. They offered to buy the arms of the soldiers in the field. Some of these arms, supplied by America, were up to date and formidable. The Kuomintang soldier, often unpaid and with no ideal to fight for, found it more attractive to exchange the weapons for cash rather than to risk his life in using them. If the soldier was thus corruptible for small sums, many of the Kuomintang officers could be bought for larger ones. The final economical capture of Peking and the north was due to a deal between the Communists and the Kuomintang general whom Chiang had left in command. In some circumstances a general who surrendered might hope for the guarantee of a command in the Communist army.

By the autumn of 1948 the Communist high command felt itself strong enough to fight the Kuomintang in an orthodox full-scale land battle; it no longer preferred guerilla war. The battle of Hsuchow lasted a month and was Chiang Kai-shek's worst defeat; comparable to that of Napoleon at Leipzig. The price he paid was the loss of his capital, Nanking, the city which had been revived from destitution by the Kuomintang and had become the symbol of the party's prosperity.

The price was greater, for as the result of defeats the unity of the Kuomintang was broken. For some time a group in the party had believed that if Chiang was removed it might be possible to come to terms with the Communists and form a coalition. Chiang was persuaded to withdraw temporarily (though the army commanders who were still loyal to him continued to take his instructions and not those of the titular government). The Communists kept his successors in play while they extended their victories and then broke off contact. Chiang Kai-shek resumed full authority, but by now he could save nothing from the wreck upon mainland China. The continuing defeats showed how hopelessly the Kuomintang had lost. It was like the collapse of the Manchus in 1911. Terrain, numbers of troops, supplies – all should have been in favour of the Kuomintang in South China, and it should have taken the Communists years to conquer the whole country even after they crossed the Yangtze and took Nanking. But no will to fight remained. By the autumn the Kuomintang lost its last positions on the mainland. All that Chiang could remove of his army was ferried over to the island of Formosa, ninety miles from the province of Fukien.*

The change for the Communists was immense. All the vast mainland of China now lay under their authority. But how were they to administer it? The Communist party was heterogeneous in origin. At the beginning in the twenties it was recruited chiefly from the intellectual and the middle class; when it shifted to the rural areas genuine peasants were added. Professional bandits also joined; the bandit was one of the oldest figures of Chinese history; it was traditional that in times of trouble the more audacious members of rural society took to the hills and became

* Even the commercial classes in Shanghai, which had flourished greatly under Chiang's rule, turned against him. In a desperate effort to end the currency inflation, he had introduced a new currency. His son, Chiang Ching-kuo, who controlled Shanghai, tried to keep it stable by forbidding speculation under the most drastic penalties. When he began to exact these penalties, the commercial classes felt that even Communism could hardly hold out more horror.

brigands; little moral blame was attached provided the bandit acted with moderation.

Almost until its final victories the Communist party remained small in number. Then it grew quickly. Its membership in 1945 was 1,210,000; in 1951 it was 5 million. The party had now the task not only of carrying on the administration and of deciding China's relations with foreign powers, but also of carrying through the great transformation in Chinese society for which Communism stands.

After the flight of Chiang Kai-shek from the mainland there was a pause while China had, technically, no central government. Then in October 1949 the new régime was proclaimed. It was set up in Peking, the old imperial capital of the Manchu dynasty, thus signifying that the mighty China of the past was being brought to life again. Nanking, the capital of the Kuomintang, became once again a provincial city.

During the months before the setting up of the new government the Communists had been negotiating with several of the small groups and parties which, without allying themselves during the civil war openly with the Communists, had opposed Chiang Kai-shek. The Communists wished that there should be the appearance of a coalition government, at least in form. The Communists therefore offered to abate a little the full Communist programme of government in return for the collaboration of these groups. An agreement was arrived at and defined in what became known as the Common Programme.

II   THE COMMUNIST STRUCTURE

THE new system of government in China, which was to affect so deeply the mind and fortunes of Asia, did not, when it first began to take shape, appear very novel or revolutionary, at least in its constitutional forms. These were copied partly from the Soviet constitution and partly from the Kuomintang state which was being replaced. As in the days of the Kuomintang, the machinery of party and state were interlocked. But now it was the totalitarian Communist party and not the mildly authoritarian Kuomintang which controlled the state. Moreover, the new state abandoned the Kuomintang principle of a separation of powers in the executive.

The details of the political system are complex. But it is now so central in the Asian scene that its structure, and also the structure of the Chinese Communist party, require to be studied in detail. They may become the model elsewhere.

The myth which is used to give reason to the Chinese system is that society consists of two orders. One is the 'touchables', comprising the poor peasants, the richer peasants whose turn to be sacrificed has not yet arrived, the urban proletariat, and any sections of the middle or upper classes whom it suits the Communists for the time being to tolerate and who are therefore classified as patriotic. These all form the ranks of the 'people'. On the other side are the 'untouchables', the supplanted ruling class, who are to be outlawed, hunted down and denied all rights. According to the myth the new institutions of the state express the will of the righteous – or victorious – part of society, the people. The institutions are therefore democratic.

All power is concentrated in the Communist party, and this, like the party in Russia, is hierarchically organized. The effective supremacy is in the Politburo, which is presided over by Mao Tse-tung. The guiding rule in the party's government is 'democratic centralism'. This means that in theory members of the party at all levels may debate policy freely until the policy is decided. Thereafter they must obey instructions and follow the party line, whatever their personal views about it may be. Much of the power of the Communist party is due to this rigid discipline. It is as well drilled as the Prussian army. The authoritarianism in the Chinese Communist party is the stronger because, although the constitution of the party provides that there shall be a Party Congress once every three years, only one has been held in the last twenty-seven years.

Side by side with the organs of the party are the organs of the state. The Organic Law, by which these are regulated, was only promulgated in 1953, and then after long preparation. The law provides for a hierarchy of assemblies, ostensibly elected by universal suffrage of those above eighteen years of age. The hierarchy extends from local rural assemblies to a National Peoples' Congress (which is indirectly elected from the lower assemblies). From these assemblies, again ostensibly by election, come at the varying levels the executive councils which carry on the executive government of the country; but by an interesting provision the decisions of each council have to be approved by the council at the next higher level. The supreme executive organ is the Central People's Governing Council, which consists of a chairman, six vice-chairmen, and fifty-six members. This delegates its powers to a State Administrative Council of twenty members. This is the nearest approach to a cabinet in the Western sense. But it operates by means of a maze of committees. The central government maintains direct control over officials down almost to the lowest level. The provincial autonomy of the Kuomintang period has disappeared.

Obviously this is an elaborate machinery, and it still has not yet been set up in full. As an interim measure the government created at various levels what were called 'all circles conferences'. These were nominated to represent various functional groups and acted as a kind of consultative assembly or sounding-board.

How the party machinery and the state machinery are related is not entirely clear. In theory it should be possible for opponents of the Communist party to be elected in the various assemblies. In fact none is. The entire machinery is controlled with complete effectiveness by the Communists. At the lower levels, it is true, there may be fairly free elections and the assemblies may be fairly representative. They may be encouraged to criticize the functioning of the administration – though not basic policies – because it is useful for the government to be kept aware of the public sentiment. But the higher the assembly the less genuinely representative.

Not that the government is monolithically Communist. From the start the leaders wished to demonstrate that the government had a national backing as well as being a party dictatorship. This fitted in with the political theories of Mao Tse-tung. In his pamphlet *On New Democracy* he said, like any orthodox Marxist, that the revolution in China must be in two stages; feudalism must be overthrown by capitalism, and capitalism must be overthrown by socialism. But he said – and this was his individual contribution to theory – that in the revolution in China the two revolutions could go on simultaneously.* The corollary was that the form of government proper to China should be a coalition of the Communist party with other patriotic and democratic parties which might co-operate in one or other revolution. These could be the urban middle class, patriotic capitalists, Communist intellectuals, and substantial farmers. ('Imperialist, feudal, and bureaucratic elements' would be excluded.) The Communist party would, of course, have primacy in the coalition. To put these ideas into practice was relatively easy. In the last days of the Kuomintang a number of splinter parties had formed as a protest against its misrule. Some of them had been started with the idea of offering a third possibility besides the Kuomintang and the Communists; but they had had no prospect of gaining mass support. Members of these parties were flattered by the invitation to join the government. They accepted, but they had no real power, though some of their individual members, including defecting generals from the Kuomintang, were given posts of responsibility. With apparent moderation the Communists published a 'Common Programme' which the minor parties had agreed upon with them. Actually it contained all the measures of Communism which Mao Tse-tung at the time thought practicable.

The bringing in of the minor parties nevertheless emphasized that there was to be a gradualness about the revolution. Some classes which full-blooded Communism would not tolerate were to continue for a time. Among these were many of the business men. Private enterprise was not to be abolished as completely and rapidly as in the Russian revolution; but the private capitalists must submit to governmental control and must not oppose the

---

* This theme has been debated for thirty years. In the twenties, during the Borodin adventure in China, it was the great controversy between Stalin and Trotsky. Stalin argued that the revolutions must be successive. Communists should therefore support bourgeois democracy in overthrowing feudalism and should go on to the communist revolution afterwards. Trotsky argued that Communism could abolish feudalism and there need be no capitalist phase. The debate is not very realist because there has been no feudal period in China such as is understood in the West.

government in any way. They could be capitalists in a socialist state, under sentence of eventual extinction, but a suspended sentence. To be safe for the time, most of them had occasionally to offer some of their possessions to the state, to pay fines cheerfully, and to admit the state to partnership in their business. On these terms even some very wealthy capitalists were tolerated and almost honoured. But the whip was cracked periodically. The sharpest cuts were in 1952 during a movement called the 'three antis' – against corruption, against bureaucracy, and against waste. During this the capitalists who had failed to satisfy the Communists were purged, and the remainder made very large subscriptions to government loans.*

A special peculiarity of the political system of Communist China is its reliance on the so-called Communist 'cadres'. These are dedicated servants of the party by whom the whole system is sustained. Their role has been well described.

'The strength of the Communist Party really lies in the selfless and efficient services rendered by the staff workers, the cadres. Cadres are usually young enthusiastic party members, sometimes even non-members who are especially designated by the party to take the lead in various governmental or party activities. The qualities required of every cadre are loyalty, obedience, initiative and ability in organizing the masses. A man of thirty is usually regarded as being too old to become a good cadre. Back in the days of the war against Japan, the Communists established a number of schools for the training of cadres. Admission was restricted to promising young candidates who showed high aptitude for profiting by training in professional, political, ideological or cultural fields. The formal education was only part of their training. The final processing they obtained through these facilities came through "learning from the masses." In simple terms this meant field work. Among the cadres, those who came from the peasant and worker classes had to take courses on cultural matters, and those with good intellectual backgrounds were required to live among the peasantry to learn the language

---

* This movement was followed by the 'Five Antis' – against graft, against tax evasion and smuggling, against theft of state economic information, against theft of state property, and against cheating in materials.

of the common people and to think in terms of their everyday living. Only after thorough training for one or two years were the cadres sent forth to do real work in the field. These cadres contributed a great deal in the military campaigns. They took over a great part of the non-combatant work, such as propaganda, mass organization, and provisional land reform. At the time that the Kuomintang finally fell, the Communists had enough trained young people on hand to incorporate 150,000 of them into the land programme of the newly liberated areas alone. Without cadres, the Communists would have had difficulty in taking and holding power. The party was simply not big enough to manage the complicated political, economic and social situation after the Communist conquest.' *

Both the Communist party and the corps of cadres have naturally been infiltrated by those whose motives were not what the leaders would wish. From time to time there are purges and mass expulsion, and recently – as the result perhaps of factional disputes within the party – there has been created a kind of special party police to watch the activities of individual cadres.

The cadres are a special force of shock troops. They are not the regular civil service. This is in process of re-formation. A part was necessarily taken over from the Kuomintang, but the service is being reorganized and indoctrinated, and it is once again to be recruited by examination instead of by patronage as under the Kuomintang. Some of the brutalities and follies of the government arise out of the very low education of both the cadres and many civil servants. A government as totalitarian as the Chinese has to maintain a vast army of officials, and it is far in excess of the number of educated men available. Although all have nominally some knowledge of the basic principles of Communism, their acquaintance with them is often hazy or perverted.

The government also relies, as a means of controlling the country, upon mass vocational organizations. There are associations for most of the main occupational groups. These discipline their members, and society is made more organic. This is not a

* From *Far Eastern Governments and Politics*, by Linebarger, Djang and Banks.

new invention of the Chinese Communists, but was copied from the new democracies of Eastern Europe.

Besides these new style instruments of government, the Chinese Red Army plays a part. A curious provision in the constitution detaches the control of the army from the national cabinet – the State Administrative Council – and puts it under a Revolutionary Military Council, which nominally comes under the Central Governing Council, but probably enjoys a good deal of autonomy. At least during the early stages of the Communist government, the army had the right to intervene in local government affairs and supersede officials. It may be that recently the powers of area commanders have been reduced. Moreover the army is carefully indoctrinated with Communism. But the Red Army may in future still give a new turn to politics in China if the civilian leaders should fall out.

The Communist leaders live withdrawn lives. The struggles inside the ruling group happen in secret. On the whole the Chinese Communist leaders have competed with each other less sharply than the Russians. The revolution has been slower to devour its children, and until last year there had apparently been no serious casualties among the topmost leaders, even though the policies had changed from time to time and with the changes some of the former grandees of the party, such as Li Li-san, had faded out. But this may be changing. Recently the government announced that Kao Kang, once the virtual dictator of Manchuria, had been expelled from the party for opposition. Refusing to admit his guilt, he had committed suicide. (Was it suicide or was he executed?) The announcement implied that Kao Kang had been joined by other fairly high personages. The result of the struggle was announced some months after it had taken place, and little light was thrown on the way in which it had been fought out. How does one group in the party oust another? What are the instruments which give it control and how does it fasten its grasp upon them? These are still mysteries.

One of the most striking characteristics of the Communist state is the passion for secrecy. All the ordinary information about the functioning of the economic and social system, such as is available to everyone in the West (even if a little labour may be needed to interpret it), is in China treated as deep secrets of state. Those who try to ferret it out are spies. In practice this is one of the preservatives of authoritarian rule. It prevents any opposition from functioning, even if one was allowed. How can there be intelligent criticism of the acts of government when so many of the acts are strict secrets?

There is of course no free press. It is true that newspapers often criticize ministries. At times they do so with heart-warming trenchancy. But it is one part of the bureaucracy criticizing another. There is no genuine criticism of the régime.

Is the Chinese Communist state a copy of the Communist model in the West? Has China, after resisting for a hundred years by various means the attacks of the western parts of Europe, ended by following bewitched the model set by the eastern half of Europe? Or is Communism in China peculiarly Chinese? Obviously the Chinese state is the product of both Asian and Western influences. It is easy to trace all manner of survivals of Chinese self-expression and tradition which make the new Chinese state very different from the U.S.S.R. Before the Communists actually came to power, it was often said that they were not real Communists at all but simply agrarian reformers who had come into existence to deal with specifically Chinese problems. Mao Tse-tung, by his strategy in the revolutionary war – by appealing to the peasants rather than the urban worker – established a pattern for revolution different from that of the West. Yet once the Chinese Communists were in power, their general concepts of the relation of Communist party and state machine have been very much like those of Western Communism. There is not much in Chinese Communism which has not appeared also among the 'New Democracies' of Europe. The thought of the leading party theorists, Mao Tse-tung and Liu Shao-chi, is very Western (of the Marxist variety) and has few traces of Chinese traditional ideas. Mao likes to use old Chinese proverbs and tags of poetry, but they point a moral which is very un-Chinese.

In the years since the Communist government came into power, some of its achievements have been spectacular and beneficial.

It was a government which had emerged out of the depths of the countryside. Its soldiers and many of its minor officials were simple peasants, and the urban Chinese of the ports, which in the previous forty years had seen governments come and go, had thought it most unlikely that they would be able to govern. When the Communist armies marched in to the cities, even some of their officers had never seen electricity and tried to light their cigarettes from electric light bulbs. They mistook refrigerators for radio, and typewriters for transmitting sets.*

Nevertheless this rustic government proved itself able to do what Chiang Kai-shek failed to do. After nearly a half century of tumult it restored the authority of the government, and re-united the country. The Chinese Empire, traditionally one of the main members in the family of nations, was alive again, and soon the outer world was almost daily to be made aware of the fact. China could no longer be left out of consideration. The day of thinking of it as decadent, with a splendid past but contemptible present, was over. The self-respect of the Chinese was thereby restored. Even those who had been anti-Communist were glad to know that foreigners in China were now living in anxiety instead of in privilege, and that the world was wondering with consternation what China would do next. The new sentiment could be seen among the Chinese overseas; the richer members of this community had every reason to fear Communism, but some, because of nationalist feeling, felt attracted by the new government.

By abolishing the capital at Nanking, and re-establishing it at Peking, the government showed symbolically that it was ending one phase and starting another. Nanking was a port which was much und he influence of Shanghai, another port, and looked across the oceans to the maritime and trading countries of the

---

* The army was amazingly well disciplined, and there was no plunder of citizens by individual soldiers.

world. Within limits it desired to associate with them and was sensitive to their opinion. Peking, on the other hand, was the old imperial capital of a land empire which regarded with anxiety and repugnance the influences coming from the sea, and looked inland over the vast spaces of China. The policy of the new government was to shift the centre of industry and power from the seaboard, where it had been artificially located during the previous half-century, to the interior.

The government stabilized the currency. That was the achievement by which it first won approval from the sceptical Chinese people upon whom it had imposed itself. For decades the almost continuous inflation had distorted normal economic life, and had fostered all the rather shady habits and activities which help people to thrive at a time of constantly rising prices. The restoration of stable currency brought relief. Its methods were unconventional, improvised, and draconian, but were nevertheless effective. This was the more remarkable coming from a government which had had little previous experience of sophisticated finance.

With the same vigour the government set about removing or lessening the corruption of officials. In nearly all Asian countries there has always been a tradition of corruption. Public office meant perquisites. Officials were not well paid and had to make ends meet. The well-timed bribe – which was often almost a conventional fee – was the emollient which made the wheels of administration turn more efficiently. In the disorders in China since 1911 the scale of corruption had increased in a monstrous way, and reform was very much needed. The surprising achievement of the Communists was to be able to induce among their party members, who were after all thoroughly Chinese, a militant and puritanical hatred of the old system. Here was one of the outstanding instances of ideas and institutions being able to change people's character. The Communist Party set out to hunt the corrupt; it disciplined its own members savagely if it caught them; it developed a steady pressure against corruption in all the administration – incidentally attaching charges of corruption to all of whom it disapproved upon other grounds.

The government was a great disciplinarian. Certainly many of the previous disorders of China had come about because of social indiscipline. The new government went to extremes. Henceforward nobody was to travel from his home without a permit. A great network of control offices would keep watch on all citizens. The government set out to change social custom by persuasion. Their success in this has also been extraordinary. People queue to enter buses, instead of fighting; they no longer leave litter about; the streets have been remarkably clean instead of remarkably dirty; personal habits have improved. This visible revolution was brought about partly by the use of the slogan, to which the Chinese people have always responded, partly by a technique of propaganda alarmingly similar to that of George Orwell's 1984.

As its authority grew, the government used the power of the state to accelerate immensely the application of modern scientific knowledge in the organization of society. It set itself to produce a large army of trained technicians – doctors, engineers, and so on – who were to be the force by which China would be modernized and transformed. Health services were vastly extended; the government claims that in its first five years five hundred million people have been vaccinated; some cities are now free of the age-old ravages of smallpox; penicillin is being manufactured. Sanitary regulations in the cities are rigorously enforced. One of the proudest boasts of the new China is that there are now no flies in the market places.

The task about which the government was most zealous was promoting industry. For all Asian peoples industry has become synonymous with modernization. National self-respect demands factories. This is partly the result of decades of propaganda which represented Asia as being degraded to be the hewer of wood and drawer of water for the West; partly because military power, by which nationalism could assert itself, demanded heavy industry. As in Russia, one of the first fruits of Communism in China was a five-year plan for industry. The project of raising a hugh industrial apparatus upon a land comparatively poor in many resources, without a skilled managerial class, with very little capital, and lacking an existing industrial base except in Manchuria, was extremely bold. It is admitted that it will take fifty years before China can catch up the advanced industrial countries.

Railway building, suspended since the Revolution in 1911, was resumed. Dykes, always the first care of an energetic government in China, were vigorously restored.

As a concomitant of industrialization, the country began to be more urbanized. One of the main social changes which has come about is the swift expansion of towns. Villages are turning into cities; parts of China have the appearance of a boom area, with all the improvisation in housing which goes with that. Because the town population is growing in size, its share of membership of the Communist Party, which the leaders have always desired to see larger, is now increasing.

There are other striking reforms, some of them indisputably successful, others justifiable attempts even if less satisfactory in results. The power of the state is being used to end age-old abuses. For examples, wives are given legal rights to maintenance and divorce which are essential if women – especially young women – are to be freed from their traditional subjection. Certainly the Marriage Reform Law may have been badly drawn up, and led to absurdities and mischief because of the fanaticism with which it was enforced. But probably the women of China are among the chief beneficiaries of the revolution. Others are the non-Chinese subject peoples on China's borderland. In the past they had been roughly used. The Communist government has shown particular interest in the advice of its anthropologists about how to handle them. There is genuine interest in their civilization, which in the past the Chinese have despised.

These are the benefits – some of them rather dubious – conferred by the Communist Party. But the revolution which has convulsed Asia did not simply result in material benefits of social modernization. There was a dark side.

13   LAND REFORM

The measure which the Chinese Communists regard as the basis of their régime is a sweeping land reform. They were aware that the grievances of the tenant farmers had been the principal means of their coming to power. In all Communist countries, land reform has been a main part of the revolutionary programme. Moreover in China there had been notable precedents of large-scale reform measures carried out in ancient times by radically minded Emperors or their ministers.

The land reform was preceded and accompanied by a very extensive literature. This appeared partly in book form, but principally as long articles in the Communist newspapers. Much that was written was of interest only for the moment, and in future will be read only by historians. Yet this literature throws a great deal of light on what the Chinese Communists were trying to do, and why they acted as they did.

The first question which it is natural to ask is what was the purpose and aim of the reform. The Chinese Communists give two answers, and it has never been authoritatively stated which was correct. The first view is that land reform was made necessary by China's urgent need – which it shares with other Oriental countries – to produce more food. The factor most responsible for the country's economic backwardness, say the theorists of this school, is the out-of-date 'feudal' organization of society, especially the landlord system. It is this which frustrates progress; if it is abolished, Chinese agriculture will transform itself and become efficient.

The rival theory may be called the political one. The emphasis is no longer on the beneficial economic effects which will result from the redistribution of land. It is now quite simply upon the need for liquidating landlords. The aim is the political one of consolidating the People's Dictatorship in the countryside. This is to be done by eliminating the landed class, which is the mortal enemy of Communism.

Theory was translated into practice with grim ruthlessness. The progress, system, and results of the reform could be studied in great detail in the Chinese press. It is worth examining just what happened.

Land reform in a village was usually carried out in four stages. 'Cadres' trained for the purpose were sent to a village. As soon as they arrived, it was cordoned off for the duration of the operation; but peasants from neighbouring villages were admitted if they came to accuse the landlords. The eye-witness accounts vary about the first thing the land reformers did when they set foot in a village. Usually they sought out the poorer peasants, pieced together the facts of the village economy, and stirred them up against the landlords, especially the more tyrannical ones. The cadres' task was to inculcate among the peasants a hatred of the landlords. General indifference or mild discord had to be replaced by irreconcilable hostility.

The Communist press gives enlightening accounts of agitators who have failed and of agitators who have succeeded. The *Yangtze Daily* holds up the proceedings in a village in Hunan as an example of what not to do. It said that the cadre in charge knew the importance of mobilizing poor peasants, but was guilty of impatience, taking no pains to stir up their political consciousness previously. He called a mass accusation meeting in which he took the chair. The story continues:

' "You are all poor peasants and farm labourers. Whatever difficulties you have had, you may now speak up." Thus the cadre opened the meeting. The peasants, entirely unprepared for the occasion, did not know what to say. They remained silent.

' "You are all poor peasants and farm labourers; you have been most heavily exploited by the landlords. You may now give utterance to the wrongs you have suffered," the chairman of the meeting shouted, somewhat worried.

'The peasants still remained silent, and the chairman got more worried.

' "You all remain silent. Can it be that you have never been exploited by the landlords? Can it be that you are not all poor peasants and farm labourers?" he went on.

'The peasants knew that they were poor and oppressed, but not knowing what to say, they did not speak up. Then they were called on one by one. 'How many *mou* of land have you got?"

"How many *mou* of land have you rented?" "What rentals did you pay?" "Have you suffered no injustice?", etc., etc.

'The peasants answered these questions accordingly, but as to the last question they did not know what to say. Finally, they spoke in one voice, "Let us adjourn the meeting. We have no complaints to make." '

Compare with this a case history of an operation which had been carefully prepared. All is different. The *Southern Daily* of Canton gives a very good instance. The reformers prepared the way by calling a meeting of the poorest peasants and landless farm-hands. They cited instances of the injustices and exploitations suffered by the peasants, and emphasized that the landed class depended for their income mainly upon rents which they did not deserve and usurious interest which was pure robbery. Next day they called another meeting and divided the peasants into many small units in order to discover on whom their hatred was centred. Two landlords, alleged to be the greatest exploiters in the village, were subsequently singled out for the opening phase of 'class-struggle attack'. The third day was spent in discussions of class discord. The peasants were again told to think who supported whom and to whom the land should really belong.

In this way the peasants began to see the light. It did not take the cadres long to convince the peasants that there was not a single landlord who was not 'heartless' and that class struggle could strike them down.

Cadres were instructed that they must never themselves take part in the attacks on the landlords. They were to direct and incite the attack: but the actual assaults must be made by the peasants themselves. The Communist leaders were very frank in explaining the reason for this rule. They said that if the cadres made the attack, and the peasants were left to look on as spectators, the sympathies of the peasants might easily be on the side of the victims and against their persecutors. It was only if the peasants themselves struck the blows that the Communists regarded them as committed to their side.

The second stage of the reform was to decide the class status of each farmer in the village. This division into classes is of great importance. In the Communist scheme the rural population falls into five categories – landlords, 'rich peasants', 'middle peasants', 'poor peasants', and landless farm hands. A landlord is a land-owner who does not work and lives upon rentals and usurious interests, 'fruits of exploitation'. The rich peasant is a landowner who puts in 'full essential labour' on his land, although he may hire labourers or rent out a portion of his holdings and collect rentals. A 'middle peasant' is generally a small landowner and renter of land who neither exploits heavily nor is heavily ex-ploited. A 'poor peasant' has little or no land or tools and pays rental for the land he tills. A landless farm hand tills the land for the landlords for wages and is thus the most heavily 'exploited' person. The 'poor peasants' and the farm hands are the chosen allies of the Communists, since because of their circumstances they are considered the most likely to be enthusiastic about land reform. But the 'middle peasants' are also to be won over.

It was at this stage of land reform that errors and confusion be-come most abundant. It was clearly not easy to determine whether a man had contributed 'essential labour', which by legal definition consisted of four months of 'principal' or heavy farm work. It was difficult to ascertain how much time anyone contributed to his farm in a year. For the smaller landowners the classification of status was often a matter of life or death. If a better-off peasant was classified as a landlord it meant total dispossession, and even a more fearful fate; but if he was classified as a rich peasant he might retain the land tilled by himself and his hired labourers. Small landowners fought desperately to obtain the status of rich peasants. The fight against being graded too high went on all down the line, and with good reason. A middle peasant, if classi-fied as a rich peasant, would lose his 'surplus' land or the land put out to lease. He would also lose his politically unprejudiced po-sition and would be looked upon as belonging to a class liable to heavy taxation. Similarly, if a 'poor peasant' was classified as a middle peasant, he lost his superior political position.

The third stage of the reform was the redistribution of property. Peasants might demand from the landlords the rentals of which they had previously been 'exploited'. The demands were some-times so excessive that they became farces. One labourer who carried water for his landlord worked out that he had been underpaid to the extent of 300,000 silver dollars or approximately £75,000 sterling in current purchasing power. In parts of Kwangtung Province the demands for refund of rent went as far back as the Manchu Dynasty, which ended over forty years ago.

At this stage violence was even more common than in the first or second stage. Torture was a general practice when the landlords failed to pay the amount demanded. As often as not torture brought results. Some landlords had hidden their property before the land reformers got at them. In one case a landlord, after sustaining four rounds of class struggle, finally submitted and surrendered over 800 silver dollars buried underground.

By the time dispossession was completed, land reform emerged from the smoke and fire of class struggle and entered a technical phase. The enemy was supposed to have been struck down. All that remained to be done was to distribute the property confiscated and allot land to the peasants.

The redistribution of land was based on the principle of giving the peasants, wherever possible, the land which they used to till. This might be added to or reduced in the interests of equality. The actual measurement of land, a task of great difficulty, was neither carried out nor advised. The rule of mass opinion was again enforced, and it was only in exceptional circumstances that measurement was undertaken.

The last stage of the land reform was more dignified. The landlords' old title deeds and contracts of lease of land were burned publicly – a symbolic funeral for 'feudalism'. Equally symbolic of the defeat of the landed class was that in some parts of the countryside landlords were ordered to kneel in surrendering their title deeds.

The reports in the Communist press make it clear that the procedure in the four stages just outlined was more often than not lost in the swell and surge of violence. Even the Communist press criticized this. 'The cadres', said one article, 'urged the landlords to give up their property, and when that failed, the cadres bound them hand and foot with ropes and beat them heavily ... when mass passion ran high, wild arrests followed ... torture was repeatedly applied to the landlords during class struggle ... this sort of noisy and riotous procedure and blind tumultuous action only scares away the masses, isolates oneself, and gives the land-lords a chance to increase their resistance.'

How extensive was the change in land ownership? No detailed statistics have been published. But some revealing figures were given by the New China News Agency in the middle of 1951. The land confiscated and requisitioned from landlords in Central and South China amounted, said the Agency, to about 40 per cent of the total arable land. In South-west China, where the landlord system was known to be particularly onerous, the amount was 60 per cent.

Such was the great tenancy reform – much advertised in its aspect of emancipating the tenant but hushed up in its more brutal aspects. How much, if at all, the peasants benefited it is hard to say. In some Communist countries the peasant, after land reform, has paid more in increased taxes to the state than he did in rent to the landlord before. The information from China is not complete enough to know whether this happened in China also.

In any case, the giving of the land to the peasant was only the first stage in the agrarian revolution. That stage was finished in 1952. By 1954 a new one had begun. This new phase, which in some ways abolished the effects of what had already been done, was collectivization, to be achieved by stages. It would take back again from the farmers what had been given to them after the spoliation of the landlords.

Long debates in the Communist party preceded the announce-ment of the new policy, and this was understandable because it was very radical. The conditions of farming in much of China was not very suitable technically for large-scale farms; its irrigated rice land is best farmed like so many small gardens. But Com-munist orthodoxy, which the Chinese Communists greatly respect even if they have a reputation for common sense and for being willing to learn by experience, requires collectivization every-where. Partly it is because a peasant population which is collecti-vized is easier to control politically, partly because the Commun-ists see great danger if in the rural districts there grows up a class of more or less contented peasant proprietors. These, according to the Communists, develop inevitably into petty capitalists, with a capitalist and conservative mentality, and they may eventually strangle the revolution and prevent the socialization of the rest of society. Presumably that was what initially had caused in Russia the decision to collectivize, and the Chinese felt themselves driven by the same reasoning.

The Communist fears were expressed frankly in an article during these debates in the *People's Daily*, the principal Communist newspaper. 'In what direction are the forces liberated by agrarian reform developing,' it asked, 'that of capitalism or that of socialism? The struggle between the increase of socialist development and incipient capitalism is becoming more and more manifest. This situation is of such a nature that it is becoming especially urgent to find a solution by various means to the question, Which of the two is going to win through in the country?'

The Chinese government, having decided in principle to take the momentous step of changing the whole basis of agriculture, has moved cautiously. The first step has been to bring farmers together in what are called mutual-aid societies. In these the farmers cultivate land in common, but for a time will retain the ownership of their individual plots, which have been pooled to form the new units. In organizing this system the Communists have been helped by various peculiar features of the traditional system in China; in many provinces it was common for all farmers to band themselves together at times when labour was urgently needed and to work as a team successively upon the land of each. The aim of the Communists is, however, to go far beyond this. Ultimately the boundary marks of the individual plots will be removed, land will be held in common, and peasants will be paid simply for their labour. The programme is being pushed with energy even if with occasional pauses for caution and consolidation. The Communists say that about 600,000 societies have so far been organized, covering about 13 per cent of all peasant families. By next year there will be a million. By the early 1960s all China will be organized.

By these means the peasantry, which will always be the largest part of the Chinese population, is being socialized. It is thus taking its full part in the Communist revolution, which its own peasant armies made possible, though they doubtless had little idea of what they were bringing into being. The peasantry is also being made to contribute notably to the Communist development of the rest of society. The great ambition of Communism is to industralize; industrialization requires capital, and that, in China, is to be raised by exactions from the farmers. These are gathered partly by means of a state monopoly which the government has set up for trading in cereals, the principal foodstuffs, and eight principal non-alimentary agricultural products, including cotton. The state demands from the peasant a return of his whole product, leaves him with what he needs for his next sowing, and buys the rest at a fixed price. If the price is low, the state makes a handsome profit, which it may use as capital for industrial investment and for trade with foreign countries in order to buy the machinery needed for industrialization. Thus, as in times past, the peasant must still bear all upon his back. Formerly it was the imperial government. To-day it is the Communist Utopia.

What have been the consequences of these policies? It is hard to know. In undertaking these great changes the Chinese government is taking risks. The population is growing; the food demand for the cities is rising. If the Chinese system is to be judged a success, a substantial increase of agricultural output is needed, and if it fails to happen, or if there should be a decline, the régime would probably face calamity. The Communists claim that output is rising but admit that it is not to the extent which they had hoped. With the return of ordered life there should certainly have been improvement in comparison with the production in the previous thirty years, when the country had been so often ravaged. There are plenty of signs of peasant discontent, among them a constant flight of peasants to the towns, which the Chinese press deplores regularly. It is hard to sort out fact from propaganda in the rumours which leak out of small peasant rebellions. Recently the government has announced that, as a concession and an incentive to the farmer to produce more, the government will leave him with a margin of his output for private trade. But whatever the mood of the farmer, whatever the immediate results in production, and whatever tactical shifts the government may make, the Communist government is likely to press on undeterred in its plans for creating a Communist and collectivized peasantry.

THE year when the land reform was at its peak was 1951. This was also the year of the great terror. The terror has been one of the outstanding features of the Chinese revolution. The same had happened in the Russian revolution and also the first French revolution. Indeed, as it unrolled, the Chinese revolution followed in a strangely close way the pattern of the French revolution.

As in France, the revolution began mildly. When the Communist government was first set up in Peking, it had surprised agreeably those who remembered the blood-curdling past of Communist governments in China and who had expected extinction. The year or two of affability which followed corresponded to the tolerant years in France of 1790 and 1791. But not everybody was reassured. 'It will be a process first of nod-the-head,' said one observant Chinese, 'then of shake-the-head, and finally of cut-off-the-head.' The phase of nodding the head amiably did not last more than a year.

The transition to terror came about, as in revolutionary France, because of war. In France the revolutionary government, beginning a crusade beyond its borders, collided with Austria and Prussia. The commander-in-chief of the foreign armies advancing on Paris issued the Coblenz decrees, threatening retribution against those who might harm the royal family in France. For China, the Coblenz decrees were the war in Korea. In October 1950 the forces of the United Nations, victorious in Korea, crossed the 38th Parallel. The government at Peking proclaimed this a threat to China; whether they really believed it or not, they said that the United Nations' army might pass on from Korea over the frontier into Manchuria and try to suppress the Communist government and restore Chiang Kai-shek. Inspired by this fear – or pretending to be inspired – the Chinese sent their own armies into Korea to rally the defeated northerners.

This was one of the most fateful dates in the modern history of the Far East. From it came the baleful sharpening of the Chinese revolution. The parallel with France continues. In France the Coblenz decrees led to the storming of the Tuileries, the overthrow of the monarchy, and the massacre of political prisoners. In China the intervention in Korea was followed by a new law against 'counter-revolutionaries' and 'secret agents'.

For the next few months China, in the drive against these alleged monsters, showed all the symptoms of political neurosis by which great societies are from time to time afflicted. It appears that the Communist party was sincerely convinced that when Chiang Kai-shek fled from the mainland he had left behind him a highly organized net of spies and subversive agents. These would remain hidden underground until Chiang Kai-shek tried to counter-attack – with American backing – and would then strike on his behalf. It is very likely that the Kuomintang did try to organize some kind of secret organization. They had done so before in the territory overrun by Japan, and the existence of secret societies which could be employed for the purpose made it easy. But the alarmed imagination of the Communists swelled to very great proportions whatever secret force existed. The Communists saw almost every non-Communist as a possible secret agent. They suspected that the agents had wormed their way even into the party. Kuomintang secret agents became the feared bogy-men of the time. No Communist leader was quite convinced that even his most familiar colleague, his secretary, his visitors, were not secret agents, ready to take the first opportunity of committing assassination. The Communists struck back; and just because the enemy was to a great extent imaginary they acted with all the more ruthlessness because they could not see their adversary or judge their real danger. Immense numbers of people were seized and thrown into prison. The qualification to be arrested was to have enjoyed any social privilege under the Kuomintang régime which might lead a man to prefer that to Communism. Landlords, former Kuomintang officers and former officials were the chief target, but the net was cast very widely. The terror was much worse in the villages than in the towns. It was country-wide. On the whole, the further a village from the capital the more savage was the proscription.

All the available large buildings – temples, Christian churches, halls – were filled up with prisoners. The overcrowding and misery has been described in many records. But gaol deliveries quickly began. The law against counter-revolutionaries provided for their trial before people's courts. The process was grim. In a village selected as a centre for trials a large concourse of peasants would be assembled. Skilful propaganda worked up their feelings. The prisoners were then produced before them; many were, in fact, reprehensible characters, local despots under whom the villages had suffered, but there were countless others who had committed no offences which would have brought them before ordinary courts, or even have exposed them to general censure. The organizers of the trial would then read out the terrible crimes of the accused, invite testimony to their offences and, turning to the people, would ask what should be done with them. The usual response, for which the gathering had been coached, was a great cry of 'Kill, kill'; and the demand was usually gratified, often upon the same spot as the trial. Trials, and sometimes even the executions, were broadcast; listeners in Hong Kong heard the shots and the screams of the dying. Such a resolve to advertise inhumanity was perhaps without parallel in history.

An attempt was made by sympathizers with Communism to represent these revolutionary people's courts as being organs which, whatever their technical shortcomings, did substantial justice. They cut through legal red tape. Yet it is hard to regard them as judicial bodies at all. No real evidence was taken. The accused could not interrogate the witnesses. No lawyers were allowed.

These proceedings have been described in many books. One among many is by an American priest in Kwangsi province. He describes how, after the crowds had gone away when an execution was over, the children would creep out and re-enact the trial and slaughter.

'They would climb on the stage and would go through a whole mock trial in perfect imitation of the real thing they had watched earlier in the day. They would force the "condemned" child to kneel, and would strike him on the back of his neck, then kick him and drag him off the stage, where a mock execution would take place, accompanied with fiendish cheers. These cold-blooded performances were watched by amused and approving soldiers.'*

This might be set side by side with the accounts of the French

* From *Calvary in China*, by Robert Greene.

aristocrats playing at executions in gaol while waiting for the real thing.

How many people died in the terror? For a long while the world was left to guesswork. Then in September 1952 Po Yi-po, the Minister of Finance, made a remarkable statement.

'In the past three years,' he said, 'we have liquidated more than two million bandits. Bandits are non-existent in China now, and the social order has become stable as never before.'

'Bandit' means anybody who possessed a little land or who was regarded by the Communists as dangerous to the régime. Po Yi-po's confession was naturally not very well regarded abroad. It was an indiscretion, and attempts were made by the Communists abroad to say that he had been misreported. 'Liquidated', it was said, meant reformed. The bandits had ceased to be bandits but had become good citizens. But the official Peking radio repeated Po Yi-po in more detail:

'In the past three years we have liquidated more than two million bandits and controlled a large number of counter-revolutionary secret agents. Now the bandits are all dead.'

That was a pretty definite assertion.

Though the worst period of the Terror was over by that time, there have since been periodical, if less ghastly, revivals. A new hunt for 'counter-revolutionaries' is being carried on at the present time.

15   FORCED LABOUR

THOUGH so many were executed, the number of those condemned to death and reprieved was still very much higher. The Chinese Communists, even during the years of the maximum terror, prided themselves upon their leniency. But leniency meant in most cases the substitution of forced labour for execution.

A little before the Communist government was set up at Peking, Mao Tse-tung had stated in principle the programme for forced labour. 'As for those belonging to reactionary classes or groups,' he said in his pamphlet *On People's Democratic Dictator-*

ship, 'after their political power has been broken, we will permit them to make a living and to reform themselves through labour into new persons. If they do not want to work, the people's State will force them to do so.'

The Common Programme of 1949 provided for compulsory 'reform through labour'. For some time not very much news came out of China about how this was being put into effect. But from time to time there were references in general statements to prisoners being engaged in water conservancy, in mines, in building roads and railways. In 1951 Lo Jui-ching, the Minister of Public Security, made a fairly explicit statement:

'The counter-revolutionaries who are condemned to death and whose sentence is suspended will be on parole for two years. During this time they will be forced to undertake corrective labour. If they really improve themselves, the government may consider commuting their death sentences to life imprisonment; and if they further improve themselves the government may consider another alleviation of punishment . . . From an economic point of view, these temporarily respited counter-revolutionaries are a labour force. By organizing them and forcing them to work for the state we shall, quite apart from giving them an opportunity to reform themselves, also contribute to certain production and reconstruction tasks.'

From this it was clear that at least to a section of the Chinese government there had come the vision, as in Russia, of organizing an immense force of labour, deprived of political and economic rights, which could be used as a principal instrument in the immense programme of reconstructing China. So many of the tasks to be done involved the changing of the face of Nature, so much depended on huge, painful endeavours by armies of labourers, that the temptation to mobilize the prisoners, political and criminal, was overwhelming. In August 1954 the system which was then operating was summed up in 'Regulations governing compulsory labour' which were ratified at once by the National People's Congress. These, it was explained, were based on similar regulations in the Soviet Union. To say the least, their seventy-seven articles are comprehensive.

Compulsory labour, it is decreed, can be exacted both from

counter-revolutionary and ordinary prisoners. 'Counter-revolutionary' in China is a loose definition. It includes not only those who engage in political opposition, but those likely to harbour dangerous thoughts and those who, though they have not engaged in sabotage, may endanger industry by sloth or folly.* They are drawn not only from the 'remnants of the shattered classes' but from the whole community, including deviationists in the Communist party. Just how the convicts are selected for forced labour is not clear. Article 36 of the regulations stipulates that the authorities in charge of labour must inspect the documents of sentence and commitment. But who does the sentencing is not explained. It seems that often it is not necessary to have been sentenced at all. There have been many references in China to 'detention houses', which, being maintained by the authorities at all levels from the central government to district government, are described as being 'mainly for detaining unsentenced convicts'. From these detention houses come, apparently, much of the labour used on road building and water conservancy.†

Those prisoners who are formally sentenced to compulsory labour have a fixed term to serve. But release at the end of the period is doubtful. If the prisoner has worked without enthusiasm, the detention can be prolonged; the prison authorities can also prolong a sentence by making application to the local People's Court. A supplementary regulation even places all prisoners at the end of their term at the disposal of the prison authorities, and

---

* In August 1954 the *People's Daily* in an article grouped as counter-revolutionaries those who 'generally dare not have recourse to open sabotage, which they carry out by double faced methods of concealment. Utilizing lawful posts, they deliberately make errors and omissions in designs and plans. They offer false data. In technical guidance they issue wrong instructions. Under the slogan of actively increasing production, they enlarge and aggravate errors, apparently raising production for the moment while ruining and destroying the entire factory or mine.' In factories operated by those who have until recently been peasants, when so much goes wrong because of inexperience, every breakdown is apparently blamed on the hidden hand of the counter-revolutionary. Every blunder is a dark political plot.

† There is a curious rule that the unsentenced prisoners must be paid for and supported by their relatives. If these are in the neighbourhood they send in food; if not, they must pay cash.

they may be required to continue in custody, or to reside where the government judges labour most needed, or to take up any employment which the government directs.

The normal labouring day for the prisoners is fixed by the regulations at nine or ten hours, but in seasonal emergency it may be extended to twelve hours.

The vast labour force which is produced by these regulations is at the service of the Economic and Finance Committees of the government at various levels. Provinces and municipalities are to set up special committees for using the labour for the most productive purposes.

Naturally the system is kept out of the eye of most visitors. But a vivid little glimpse was obtained by one of the journalists who in 1954 accompanied the mission of the British Labour Party to China. He visited a gaol where prisoners under the delayed sentence of death were engaged on the two-year test period during which it would be decided if the sentence could be commuted to life imprisonment:

'We went into the factories, the sock factory, the dye rooms, the bookbinding and printing shops. Men, and women too, were working with the brittle intensity of a machine, arms like the flying shuttle of a sewing machine, pistons for legs. They were making socks and books. Their work was not unduly heavy. But they made their socks with dedicated speed and concentration, performing repeated motions countless times a minute, mindless of us, of the Deputy Governor, of their neighbours, mindless of any single thought or sensation save the particular primitive muscular function they were performing. "We have no trouble with them at all," said the Deputy Governor.'*

16 BRAIN-WASHING

SOME of the counter-revolutionaries were not sent to forced labour, at least immediately, but became instead the target for

* From *No Flies in China* by G. S. Gale.

the Communist zeal in converting and indoctrinating. Special institutions were created in which the proselytizing could be carried on. They have been described by a young Christian missionary, Geoffrey Bull, who suffered in them for three years.

Bull was an English evangelist with such rather naïve ardour that he went soon after the end of the war to Tibet in the hope of converting the Lamaists, who have been impervious to all missionaries. When Tibet was conquered by the Chinese Communists he fell into their hands. It was irony that Bull, a determined proselytizer of a type rare to-day in the West, went to the East to evangelize, and was there taken hold of by evangelists no less resolute than himself, who were bent on wrestling for his soul. From the time he fell into their power they seemed to be set not so much on eliminating a possible spy (which they certainly believed him to be) as on converting him and regenerating him. At their disposal were means such as Christians have not employed since the days of the Inquisition. Their instruments are a variety of prisons, each adapted to a different purpose, a technique of spiritual sapping, and the sanction of possible execution or confinement in conditions of 'special bitterness'. Bull described his experiences in a remarkable book called *When Iron Gates Yield*.

Bull was held captive for three years. The first part he spent in an ordinary detention centre at Chinkging in West China. There he was interrogated in a more or less straightforward way (though under threat of execution) about political matters. The Chinese wanted, not unnaturally, to know what he had been doing in Tibet. He made a clean breast; in one respect he had connived at political activity. He had had knowledge of, though he had not approved, the action of a missionary colleague in going to India to try to rouse sympathy for the Tibetan chieftains, who had shown themselves tolerant of Christianity. When the Communists were fairly satisfied that they had gained from him all he could tell in this matter, he was asked, in filling in a questionnaire about 'thought reform', to describe the changes in outlook which he had undergone. He wrote:

'If communism uses the power of the new State to lead millions away from God and down to hell, then it is more than a monster;

109

it is a virus wreaking death in the souls of men and is more terrible than any imperialism that has yet arisen.'

The interest of the Communists thereupon changed. The Communist task was to redeem an errant soul. For the purpose Bull was sent to another prison on the Tibetan borderland; and here he remained for two years and two months. His experiences were peculiar. The prison, though bristling with soldiers with tommy-guns, was less a penitentiary than a nightmare caricature of a seminary. Only Kafka has imagined anything at once so bizarre and sinister.

'The Communists,' writes Bull, 'view such institutions as hospitals. The prisoners are men maimed in mind by poisonous reactionary philosophies and false social concepts. They are cared for by officials, who are viewed as doctors. The symptoms of the patients, some of whom are in a very serious condition and may eventually have to be destroyed as being unfit for social life, are collected by warders, cell leaders, and officials. These are analysed and the medicines, such as suitable books, special conversations, struggle meetings, further solitary confinement, chains and handcuffs, or a "reform through labour camp", are applied as the groups of "doctors" decree.'

The treatment of Bull began with solitary confinement and the supply of Communist pamphlets, written for mass consumption. Sometimes, for interrogation about his opinions, he would be summoned to a macabre courtroom. Behind a large black table three or four officials sat like sphinxes. Bull had to sit in front of them on a tiny stool a few inches high. The slightest movement and a guard would shout him to stillness. Interrogation was carried on in an icy atmosphere. Nobody ever smiled. A large slogan on the wall described the Government's policy: 'Confess your crime and you live. Hide it and you die. This is suppression and leniency combined.' It was a maxim of the court never to make precise what it required from the prisoner, or what it accused him of. The prisoner had to achieve his salvation by self-analysis. When he lighted on the appropriate formulas he had made progress.

After a time Bull was put in a cell with other prisoners. They were called 'fellow-students'. Now the emphasis was on group discussions, carried on under the presidency of a cell leader, who was a prisoner who had given satisfactory evidence that he wished to become progressive. Bull gives an extraordianry picture of the fervour which many of his fellow-prisoners were by this time showing for propagating the new Communist doctrines. They wrestled with their comrades who remained recalcitrant with even more zeal than the officials had done. They even hated them with fury, though this was veiled in the phrase that 'the fellow-student needs our help'. Those already converted tumbled over themselves in their eulogies of the new doctrine. The incentive was the prospect of being passed on to a 'reform through labour' camp and thence to release.

For those who made little progress special methods were employed. They would be handcuffed and subjected to perhaps a week's almost continuous argument, with hardly an hour or two for sleep. They would be confronted in debate with large assemblies of the converted, called 'struggle meetings', and there was a system of expostulation known as the 'squeeze tooth-paste method'. It was pointed out to them that if they persisted in reactionary thinking they would simply be crushed by the onward march of the masses. Their fellow-prisoners would storm at them hysterically and urge the officials to use violence. When several 'struggle meetings' were being held simultaneously the noise in the prison was like bedlam. The account reads like one of the madmen scenes in an Elizabethan drama.*

Regular self-criticism was expected from all prisoners. The safest thing was to comply, but to be trivial. Bull gives what he describes as a typical example.

'As to the daily life,' says a prudent prisoner, 'I must confess that this week in mopping the floor I did not do as well as I might. This is because my thoughts are not sufficiently concentrated on the daily routine. I am thinking all the while of my case.

* Some of the prisoners not unnaturally went mad. 'The insane ones,' says Mr Bull, 'I saw on occasions. It was heartbreaking to see them. One was kept most of the while in chains. He never washed but lived alone in a far corner among filthy rags. His great cry was for execution. One day when the guard would not let him get a drink from an urn of water used for washing, he bellowed out, "You won't let me get a drink, you won't let me be executed, and you won't let me commit suicide." '

I must correct this in future. I must be for ever struggling against self-centredness, which is the besetting sin of the bourgeoisie, and seek to establish proletariat thinking which emphasizes the life of the masses. It is obvious in many things I have not changed my class standpoint. I will be glad for any opinions which fellow-students can express in regard to my many faults.

From time to time a confession meeting was held for the entire prison. On these occasions prisoners had to describe all the regulations they had transgressed in the previous six months. Often as a result there was a reshuffle. Cell leaders were degraded, and others elevated in their place.

It is hard to know why Bull was finally released from his torment and sent to South-west China and deported. His own view is that it was the result of prayer of Christian congregations abroad who knew of his plight. Though he complied a little with what was required, he never bowed his knee to the Marxist Rimmon. A strange feature was that his persecutors had apparently little idea of how their conduct must appear. When they let him go they said – it seems with sincerity – that they hoped he would carry away good thoughts of Communist China.

17   THE JUDICIARY

MARXIST theory is that the chief purpose of the judiciary of any régime is, not to do justice between disputants or safeguard the rights of the individual, but to defend the supremacy of the governing class. The Chinese Communists follow this theory in full.

The Organic Law is sketchy about the judiciary. It provides for a People's Procurator General's Office, a Codification Commission, and a Ministry of Justice. But it does not determine in close detail the structure of the system. The chief component is the so-called People's Courts. People's Courts are intended to act rapidly and to be free from legalism and professional lawyers. They are assemblies of local people, which may run into thousands, presided over by a government official, who may or may not be legally trained. In the proceedings of these courts, much of the initiative is supposed to come from the people, though the general direction is given by the presiding officer. The verdicts and the sentences are supposed to proceed from common sense as much as from law. By a decree of July 1950, People's Courts were empowered to pass the death sentence on bandits, counter-revolutionaries, saboteurs, and Kuomintang agents. They were the main legal instrument in the great terror.

Besides the People's Courts there exist Military Courts for use against counter-revolutionaries, and People's Tribunals for deciding nearly all matters rising out of the land reforms. A curious branch of the judiciary is the so-called Comrade Tribunals. These exist in important factories and mines. They are defined by the government as 'mass organizations to combat violations of labour discipline'. They lead the workers to 'ideological self-education and self-enlightenment'. Apparently these courts can give a wide range of punishments for negligence or other similar offences.

All these courts are concerned chiefly with the business of the government in disciplining and controlling its subjects. For doing justice in disputes between citizens there are separate institutions. These are Mediation Committees, of which 155,000 have been set up. In trying to persuade citizens to compose their differences, the Communists are following the tradition of the Chinese Empire. Governments in China have always preferred that citizens should be made to agree among themselves rather than that the magistrate should give judgement.

The Communist ideas of the nature of law were not immediately accepted by all Chinese judges. Some of these tried to keep alive more normal concepts of justice. The older ideas continued to flourish. This led to official rebukes. For example, Shen Chun-jo, the President of the Supreme People's Court, said in a major declaration of policy:

'Not a few cadres do not see clearly the correct relationship between law and politics. They erroneously oppose the one to the other, or put the law above politics, thereby in effect divorcing the judiciary from politics.'

Perhaps in the last resort it is by its administration of justice that a society is best judged. It is easy to expose the hypocrisy of some Western writings about justice. Undoubtedly the law in a state serves to a great extent the circles which hold power; and the judiciary, in sensitive contact with these circles, may interpret the law with a bias. But nowhere is there the same unapologetic and thorough going use of the law as a political weapon which is now boasted of in China. The lack of concealment by the Chinese is surely surprising.

18   THE INTELLIGENTSIA

SOME of the leaders of the Chinese Communist Party were genuine working men and peasants. Mao Tse-tung was a farmer's son. But many of the prime leaders and many of the cadres came from the intelligentsia. The Communist Party had been founded by the intelligentsia. The revolution was shaped by it. Without the intelligentsia the peasant insurrection, which in any case might have happened because of the misery of modern China, would have petered out in banditry like so many expressions of peasant despair in the past. The intelligentsia took hold of it and used it as a means of creating the Communist state.

The Communist movement was served by the intelligentsia because it catered for their needs. In the Kuomintang period they had been extremely unhappy. They felt themselves isolated from the mass of the people, and powerless to guide the fortunes of their country. Communism gave them the opportunity of action. But as Communism provided them with a solace, it also exacted a price. This price was a transformation of their psychology.

Portraying the character of the Chinese intelligentsia has been a routine activity of all writers on East Asia during the past century. Naturally they have differed in their estimates. But in general it has been agreed that the typical educated Chinese was above all very sceptical. He was the product of an old civilization which had made him shrewd. He knew the motives of men, and the comic predicaments which uncontrollable fate often brought about. He thought that no simple remedies would make human life much more palatable. He believed in the importance of maintaining traditional forms which disguised the precariousness of life. He was a hedonist. He tolerated eccentricities in others. He liked gossip. He thought that if some dubious practices in the state had been current for generations, there was little point in protesting against them. Conforming to custom, whether good or moderately bad, saved much trouble. He felt no call to try to reform the world, nor did he think that it was a particularly bad place, though he probably thought that he himself had been dealt with unjustly. As for religion and systems of belief, he was an eclectic, and was willing to believe even contradictories if there seemed to be any likely advantage in doing so.

That is not the portrait of a fanatic. It was the character of the ordinary educated Chinese only a short while ago; it is the character of a great number of Chinese to-day who live outside China. But in China itself the effort is now being made to change the character radically. If any parallel to the new discipline in China can be found, it is perhaps that in England in the seventeenth century as the result of Puritanism.

The intelligentsia is now supposed to be orthodox. It must no longer be sceptical. And a large section has allowed itself to be indoctrinated. Partly this is a cynical surrender, with the object of buying security in the new society. Communist China still honours scholars, provided they are orthodox, and university professors and writers enjoy a very privileged economic position.* Partly it is a surrender to bring spiritual peace by abandoning the restless criticism and self-torment of the life of rationalism, and by submitting to the most complete intellectual dictation yet practised in the world. 'Dogma,' says Mao Tse-tung, 'is no better than cow-dung.' Yet the Chinese Communist system is based through and through on dogma, and on its little brother, the slogan.

The official view about literature and art was stated by Mao Tse-tung in a lecture – which was to become famous – which he gave in Yenan in 1942 when the Communists were still a struggling opposition. In this there occurs the following pregnant passage:

'Will not Marxism-Leninism then destroy the creative spirit?
Oh, yes, it will. It will destroy ... the creative spirit that is rooted

* A professor is paid about three times as much as a middle grade official.

in liberalism, individualism, abstractionism, the creative spirit that stands for art-for-art's sake. . . . It will destroy any brand of creative spirit which is not of the masses and of the proletariat. And is it not right that these brands of creative spirit should be destroyed as far as proletarian writers and artists are concerned? I think so. They should be extirpated to make room for the new.'

These are rather startling observations, and there has been some controversy about whether they have been properly translated. But the version given has been printed in different countries by Communist publishing houses and probably reflects Mao's true view. It is not quite as simple as it may at first seem. He does not say that all the works of the past are to be despised or condemned. The Communist government has made rather a point of praising the classical literatures, in Chinese and other languages, and has even arranged for a complete Chinese translation of Shakespeare. Molière is much prized and every possible centenary of writers is lavishly celebrated. But what is past is past, and to-day the only writing which is to be tolerated is that according to the Communist prescription.

Many intellectuals were willing to surrender. Some were swept off their feet by enthusiasm in the early days of the revolution, as often happens in revolutions – and some, if they did not accept the new ideals in their hearts, were willing to conform outwardly, though in private they ridiculed and grumbled. At first these were treated indulgently. Their support, even if given with reservations, was useful. But presently the government began to insist that the surrender should be unconditional. In 1951 it urged the intellectuals to shrive themselves. Some 15,000 writers and artists did so, and recorded that they had become much more genuinely Marxist in their outlook. 'Brain-washing' had begun. This is a process in which intellectuals (and also, reaching down, the less intellectual), under alert observation by full-blooded Communists, are set to criticize one another, to expose the shams, errors, and turpitude of their bourgeois attitudes, and to proclaim their new-birth through the acceptance of the philosophies of Marxism and materialism. Throughout the land, little groups came together to conduct these masochistic rites. Many of those taking part came unwillingly and resentfully; the atmosphere of revivalism finally overcame them, and broke down their resistance, so that they obtained a perverted pleasure in confession. Some of the most distinguished literati in China disgraced themselves by their self-abasement, and by their repudiation of the standards by which they had formerly lived. Sons denounced fathers. There was competition in describing the contamination suffered from America. Those who knew the Chinese beforehand might well have supposed that they were the last people who would be swept by the vulgar emotions of the conventicle, but they were wrong. Certainly the strain put upon them was great. Prolonged pressure, nagging, glittering material inducement for submission, threat of penury or worse for refusal, moral exhortation, the appeal of comrades, the slow operation of an atmosphere in which conformism was natural, easy and honoured – all came into play. One of the achievements of the Chinese revolution is to have discovered, or practised, effective new techniques for breaking the human will. The brain-washing on a nation-wide scale was one of the strangest indignities to which an intelligentsia has ever been submitted.

The results are shown in the intellectual life of the new China. 'It is perhaps safe to say,' says one observer, 'that in the years between 1949 and 1953 the Chinese Communists performed the equivalent of a pre-frontal lobotomy on the intellectuals whom they controlled.' The scientists may have been the least affected. Science can be conducted by compartments of the mind, and doubtless important discoveries are being made in the Chinese laboratories, which are well financed. But in the life of speculation, imagination, and criticism, all is waste. Nothing is being written above the level of propaganda. In fiction, the stock characters become wearisome – the wicked landlord, the secret enemy agent, the heroic Communist.

Mr James Cameron, the chief foreign correspondent of the *News Chronicle*, describes in his book *Mandarin Red* an interview which he had recently with Tsao Yu, one of the principal dramatists. The conversation was revealing:

' "I would venture," said Tsao Yu, "to say that Shakespeare was quite progressive *at his time*. Perhaps his themes did largely ignore the great mass of workers, but without doubt he was

making use of his princes and people symbolically. .... As I see it, Shakespeare advocated the centralization of power and government. As we know now, it was a bad idea, as things turned out, but at the time it seemed a good thing because ..."
He reached out two fingers and extricated a reason from the air, "... it would help production."

'He gained confidence: the debate that had begun so creakingly grew warmer.

' "That is it, good for production," he said. "Take *Romeo and Juliet*, a beautiful play. Its theme may seem pretty stupid now, but at the time I feel sure it had quite a valuable message."

' "Such as advocating a Marriage Reform Law?" I asked.

' "Oh, very good," cried Tsao Yu, slapping his knee. "Oh excellent, I should have thought of that. Naturally this is what it does do. But what I did have in mind was the play's exposure of feudalism, the uneconomic effect of these rivalries between politically important families. .... Similarly Shakespeare wrote *Hamlet* to expose the neurotic tendencies in royal households – a good anti-monarchist theme." '

Tsao Yu admitted that all was not well with contemporary drama in China. Romance and humour were lacking. 'We are having many committee meetings,' he said, 'to find a fashion of introducing humour into our plays.'

The need of managing literature and the masses is taken so seriously that authors who write about factories, collective farms, and the new institutions are encouraged to submit their work to the censorship of the people of the units which they are describing. Judged by the results it is not a very good method.

During the present year the government has given a new and hard turn to the screw. It began with the unmasking of a not very distinguished but combative and obstinate magazine editor named Hu Feng. He was elevated into a symbol of all that was still wrong with the intellectuals. He was denounced, hounded, dismissed from all office, arrested; then he disappeared. His private letters, in an edited form, were published to show that he, and his clique, had been counter-revolutionaries. The swathe of the new persecution was wide. Mass meetings were held all over the country to demand vigilance against the intellectual counter-revolutionaries. Professional associations demanded their punishment.

Why was the attack sharpened? It was curiously timed because it coincided with the relaxing of social tension in Russia. Two reasons were given officially. One was that thought reform was essential as part of the new, intensified effort at rapid industrialization. It would make China produce more – though why this should happen was not explained – and it was a necessary part of the Five Year Plan. The second reason was more interesting. The Communists had apparently been dwelling upon the ultimate consequences of mass education. There had opened before them the vista of a vast population reading the works not of Maoism but of typical Chinese intellectuals, still at heart unregenerate, still able, without sneering too overtly, to teach the rest to sneer. There was great danger in it, and the Communist leaders seem to have decided that the intellectual leaders of the nation must be made harmless before the new schools had done their work and had turned out the new reading public. Satisfactorily indoctrinated cadres must be the intellectual guides of the rest of the country. Hu Feng and his kind must be destroyed as a warning to all carping, critical fellows. Literature must be replaced by dogma. Assent was to be absolute, without the civil leer. There must be no more furtive criticism, no more underground war of gossip, no more holding back from complete acceptance of the new civilization, no more ambivalence.

The intelligentsia has changed in other ways. The extreme politeness which it once practised is now often systematically avoided, though it may crop out now and then by force of habit. It is on its guard against its traditional preoccupation with face – with saving its own face and that of others. These new habits may have advantages, even if they made China less pleasant to live in. They make the administration more efficient.*

An intelligentsia broken and subservient makes China a dull or rather sinister country for the visitor. It explains the strange atmosphere which has repelled so many recent travellers, even those who are impressed by the obvious material achievements of the government. A revolution, begun partly because of the

* A cult of rough clothes and general untidying which existed in the first years of Communism is apparently becoming unfashionable.

malaise of the intelligentsia, is ending – not for the first time in the history of revolutions – in a sharper discipline of the intelligentsia than has been known before.

The present generation of the intelligentsia may be the last, at least of the intelligentsia as it has been known hitherto. The intelligentsia are bred in the university; and one of the radical measures of the revolution has been university reform. Much is said about the solicitude of the government for higher education, and the amounts of money which it is spending, and the opening of the doors of the university to the poorest classes. But the universities are being converted into technical institutes instead of centres for critical and speculative studies. True, Chinese universities before the revolution had plenty of grave faults, just as those in India and the non-Communist countries of Asia do to-day. Most of them were rather poor copies of the universities of the West. But they did produce a number of men of critical and sceptical intelligence. The destruction of the old ideals of the university is one of the worst acts of vandalism by the Communists. The new institutes will produce men who may be very competent technically, but who will not be at home in the free pursuit of ideas.

19   GRANDEUR AND MISERY

THE last chapters have presented the darker side of the Chinese revolution. The more glittering side must not be regarded as of less importance. The country has been strengthened after so many decades of collapse. Revolutionary social changes have begun, some of them obviously beneficial. Science is for the first time being effectively used in the country in the relief of poverty. There is little doubt that the majority of the people, even if they dislike many of the policies of the government, do not regard it as intolerable and are content to give it the obedience which it requires. No organized opposition exists; thus far the government is stable. Many of the younger generation, not necessarily members of the Communist party, even feel for it an emotional warmth. The years before the triumph of Communism seem in retrospect so squalid and shameful that few Chinese would like to have them back.

Yet, when all this is remembered, the spectacle of China to-day is immensely saddening. Here is the end of a half a century of revolution at whose start it was hoped that China, while modernizing itself technically, would also develop a liberal and representative system of government, which seemed so well cut out for the essentially liberal and sophisticated character of the Chinese.

Among the visitors to China, who have increased in numbers in the last year or two, the impression is nearly always the same. On the one side are the imposing material works, the sweeping social changes, brought about by a semi-military organization of society; on the other side is a people regimented and disciplined in a way which denies China all claim to be considered a good society. Here are the reflections of an Indian socialist, Mr Brajkishore Shastri, looking at one of the great river projects. The peoples of South Asia sometimes feel that China may have more to offer as an example because its starting point in its economic problems is the same as theirs. Mr Shastri's conclusion was that China was a terrible warning.

'About 5,000 labourers were at work. Every piece of work, from breaking stones to cutting a tunnel or removing rocks, was being done by man's bare hands. What man can do with grit and determination and through manual labour, this sight gave us some idea of it. I mused for a while. If our government emulated this example it would in no time be able to reduce its dependence on foreign capital; there is so much human labour lying unutilized in our country. But the way I saw these Chinese labourers being driven to work evoked a stronger emotion in me than a desire for emulation or pity; I was plainly horrified. After all, a human being is not a beast. Even for reconstructing a country he should not be used as a tool of convenience.'*

* Mr Shastri found irksome the reception given to the visitors by the Liberation Army's Cultural Corps. 'In India even the best of hotels could hardly afford such a sumptuous lunch. The mocking incongruity of the spectacle of men at subsistence level being driven to break stones and cut tunnels across mountains, on the one hand, and this abandon and gaiety at the lunch table, on the other, kept buzzing in my brain.'

Here, in short, was the means by which Pharaoh built the Pyramids. China, the new pyramid, the new wonder of the world, was to be the great industrialized nation, immensely strong militarily, increasingly impressive to the rest of the world. But for the generation which builds it the suffering spent upon it is of at least as much moment as the thing which is built.

Chinese Communists may, of course, argue that the state of society and government into which China has now moved was foreordained by the course of history, and that it is useless to condemn it. By Marxist theory, every society evolves by inner necessity through its different phases, and the end phase is Communism. China has reached that phase already, and the other countries of the world are destined to follow.

This conception of an inevitable march of history carrying all in the end to Communism sustains very effectively the morale of Communists everywhere. The strong appeal of Marxism to the intelligentsia of Asia to-day is that it appears to explain to them the state reached in the evolution of their society and the forms which it must inevitably take in the future. This has the effect of buoying them up in day-to-day life, convincing them that they are being carried along by the great wave of the time. But is the new society of China really what Marx expected in a Communist state, and is the revolution in China following the Marxist pattern?

An American scholar, Dr Karl Wittfogel, probably the most percipient historian of the Chinese social structure, argues that the developments in China are not conforming at all to the model described in *Das Kapital*. The theory of most Marxists to-day, in which the Chinese concur, is that all human societies are destined to evolve in a uniform way, passing (because of the momentum of internal contradictions) from the phase of slavery through a feudal phase into the *bourgeois* liberal phase and thence into socialism. Certain variants have occurred, it is true, due to historical accident; for example, it is agreed that Western imperialism in Asia introduced there the complication of a colonial phase which was itself one of the dissolvents of feudalism. But that there is general uniformity is not questioned.

Dr Wittfogel has recalled that Marx himself did not accept this simple scheme. The evolving society which he describes in *Das Kapital* is a Western pattern. Marx recognized that another pattern existed, which he called Asiatic society. This is a society which does not necessarily evolve. It can stagnate for centuries. In a society of this kind the population was dispersed, living mostly in small villages; and the despotic government had entire control of production, revenue, property and social relations. This Asiatic society filled Marx with repugnance. He became haunted by the fear that Western society, in the process of passing through revolution, might decline into the Asiatic form and become stagnant. Lenin inherited the idea and the fear, and gave repeated expression to it, at least until 1917. So alarmed was he that, in order to guard against the intrusion of Asian forms of government, he urged at one time that after the revolution there should be no bureaucracy, no standing army, and no police. Of course the actual possession of power led him after 1917 to change his ideas. But the Marxist theory remains.

Dr Wittfogel's conclusions are more alarming than those of Marx and of the earlier Lenin. The new society in China, he says, is different from the dynamic Western society, but also it is different from the Asiatic civilization as Marx conceived it. Industrialization, the collectivization of agriculture, and new techniques in propaganda and police control give the government a power over society greater than was ever known before in any despotism. What exists in China to-day is therefore not simply a revival of 'Asiatic society'. 'Going far beyond what Lenin called an "Asiatic restoration",' says Dr Wittfogel, 'it proceeds, unevenly but steadily, towards a political, social and economic conformation that can indeed be designated as a system of general slavery.'

It is this which gives the Chinese revolution its terrible importance in the history of our time. Chinese Communism requires that all men's thoughts and hearts should lie open to them. Thought control, with which the Japanese had tentatively experimented before and during the war, is for the Chinese a matter of burning concern.

The Chinese system is based ultimately on ethics, and to say that these are 'materialist' is nonsense. They demand self-sacrifice, restraint and the austere life. Chinese Communism is based on

123

morals, but on perverted and mad morals – perverted chiefly because of the denial of freedom. A political system must in the long run be judged by whether it is possible for men living under it to develop their faculties in a balanced way. (A society must, of course, be fairly prosperous in material things if its citizens are to live the good life.) Chinese Communism, if it continues, is likely to produce a nation of men who have ceased to be critical and who have lost freedom of thought and dignity. The inhumanity of the Chinese system may prove its greatest weakness: and by inhumanity is meant not cruelty but its nonconformity to the natural self-expression of the human mind.

The governing ideas of the Chinese leaders may recall a passage from Dostoevsky in *The Brothers Karamazov*. This is the speech of the Grand Inquisitor:

'No science will give men bread as long as they remain free. Men will understand at last that freedom and bread enough for all are inconceivable together. They will become convinced too that they can never be free, for they are weak, vicious, worthless and rebellious. ... We shall triumph and then we shall plan the universal happiness of man. We shall persuade them that they can only become free when they renounce their freedom to us and submit to us. We shall set them to work, but in their leisure hours we shall make their life like a child's game, with children's songs and innocent dances. We shall tell them that every sin is expiated if it is done with our permission. They will have no secrets from us. The most painful secrets of their conscience, all, all they will bring to us, and we shall have an answer for them. And all will be happy, all the millions of creatures except the hundred thousand who rule over them.' This was Dostoevsky's expectation in Europe, but how surprised he would have been to see his prophecy coming true in China, a country which in his time was regarded as essentially a land of scepticism.

PART THREE

Succession States

*T*HE *history in Asia itself during the eight years since 1947, though complex, has seemed to have a clear pattern, rather unusual in the affairs of humanity, which are generally so confused.*

There has developed a competition carried on between China and India, the two greatest land powers in Asia, between the institutions of totalitarian Communism and those of a free society. On India's side the competition was not desired. Events brought it about. But it was clear that India had become, involuntarily, the ship of state whose voyage and fate much of the liberal part of the world was watching with mixed anxiety, relief and hope.

*In 1947 the world had to become aware that in population India was the largest of all the democracies. Under its new constitution the electorate numbered 176 millions. There was drama in the contrast between the spectacle which had existed in the years between the wars, when throughout the world parliament after parliament was being subverted and parliamentary government seemed a lost cause, and the spectacle in the post-war world, when India – and some other Asian countries – took their place as full-fledged democracies. It was dramatic, too, that a form of government which in its present shape had evolved comparatively recently in Europe had spread so rapidly to the East: the mobility of political ideas is greater than is often realized.**

At first glance it could seem that the experiment in India, however brave and magnificent, was doomed to fail. India is such a huge territory that a strong authoritarian government has usually seemed the best means of holding it together. It was multilingual. The great

---

* Parliamentary democracy in Britain has a history going back for many centuries, but its present form came into being only three generations ago.

*majority of people were illiterate. It was depressingly poor. Demo-
cracy was unknown in its traditions, except perhaps in the villages.*

*Yet between 1947 and 1955 India has governed itself with re-
markable smoothness by means of these parliamentary institutions.
Its democracy has been of the most liberal variety. The rights of the
subject have been amply protected by the courts. Perhaps India has
been lucky. Perhaps unusually good monsoons put the people in an
unusually good humour. Perhaps the strains have so far been much less
than those which are to come later. But at least, on the basis of these
first eight years, it seems possible that India in the foreseeable future
may be able to continue to carry on its affairs by a parliamentary
system broadly similar to that of the Commonwealth countries.*

*During the same period the other succession states of the British
Empire in Asia – Pakistan, Burma, and Ceylon – have similarly
tried to operate the democratic system.* So has Indonesia, the succession state of the Netherlands East Indies.† The difficulties of their
experiment are also not generally understood. Most of these countries have what is called plural societies – societies in which separate
racial or religious communities exist side by side but do not form a
real organic unity. Of all the impediments to democracy this has
often proved one of the chief.*

*The experience in Pakistan and South-east Asia has been less re-
assuring than in India. But in its different countries democracy is
still the accepted ideal. And as long as the parliamentary system is
succeeding in India the counter-attractions of China and its rival
system need not prevail.*

20 INDIA SINCE INDEPENDENCE

Wʜᴀᴛ was India's record in its first years of independence?

The first question which it had to decide was whether it wanted
continuity with what had been started under the British Raj –

---

* Malaya is now to follow.

† It is not always realized how large these countries are. Indonesia has a
population of 78 million.

whether the parliamentary and democratic state was really the proper form of government for India.

There were those who said that it was not. Many of the Gandhians in Congress disliked the modern state – its impersonality, the gap between subject and government, the dependence of a parliamentary system upon a civil service. This civil service was especially repugnant to them because civil service had meant foreign rule. After national revolution they wanted traditional Indian institutions, not institutions borrowed from the West; and among these their hopes centred on the age-old institution of the village council, the panchayat, which certainly had had admirable qualities, though in the hazy or romantic thought of the nationalists it was idealized. The true Gandhian wished India to be dissolved into its villages; the elaborate structure built by the British to be demolished; factories to be closed; the great towns, if possible, dispersed; the army and police demobilized and replaced by village constables. Since the huge majority of the population were peasants, India should be a federation of panchayats, with perhaps a central parliament, but one operating in Indian ways and not according to the procedure of Westminster. India's affairs would be run not by modern-looking men sitting in urban parliaments and secretariats and deciding at long range the fate of villagers about whom they knew nothing, but by dhoti-clad figures sitting in council under mango trees, debating placidly and deliberately limiting their range of interest to what concerned the simple life of the peasant.

The Gandhians were, however, overruled. The Congress decided that there should be no break in continuity. Emancipation thus meant not revolution but the consummation of the British endeavour to develop the liberal parliamentary society. Perhaps there was too much continuity. Perhaps the very orderliness of the evolution, the lack of dramatic upheaval, may cause trouble in the future. Some nations, like individuals, require occasional crises and explosions for their spiritual health, and if they do not take place at one time worse may happen later.

But, whatever the future holds for India, at present India offers a spectacle of a liberal society functioning elaborately and also remarkably smoothly, in most vivid contrast to what was forecast by some who had opposed the handing over of power by the British as premature. Constitutional governments, active parliaments (with spirit, form and details nearly all borrowed from Westminster), the rule of law, very extensive personal liberties, trade unions with growing influence and self-confidence – all these take the eye upon even the briefest inspection of the country to-day. Not one of these elements is to be found in China or any of the Communist countries.

It was, of course, not all smooth sailing. There has been crisis and violence. But the worst of these incidents all happened within the twelve months after the transfer of power, which could not but be profoundly unsettling.*

The laying down of British power had been accompanied by the partition of the Indian sub-continent into two states – India and Pakistan. Over the long run this was to prove the salvation of India, for in the last two years of the British Raj tension between Hindus and Moslems had become unbearable; if the British had quit India with the sub-continent still undivided, civil war between them would probably have been unavoidable. The secession of the predominantly Moslem areas to form Pakistan thus actually strengthened India; the discord between the two communities was the one friction which could not have been overcome. But though it was an act of wisdom to accept the division, and though the division was to bring great rewards in the future, the immediate consequences were not at all beneficial. They were terrifying and daunting. They were the explosion and bloodshed in the Punjab on the borderland between the two new states.

The explosion came at the end of a long period of nervous excitement and a war of nerves between the communities. On the Pakistan side of the border the Moslems in the villages, and in the towns also, turned on their Sikh and Hindu neighbours, and on the Indian side the Sikhs and Hindus murdered the Moslems. How many perished will never be known for certain. The best estimate is that there may have been as many as four or five mil-

* The twelve months before the transfer of power were nearly as unsettled as those after. There were terrible communal riots in Bengal. These have been described vividly in a book by General Sir Francis Tuker, *While Memory Serves.*

lion on either side of the frontier. The massacre was spontaneous, the result of frenzy sweeping the peoples, though some political leaders took a part in fanning the flames.

Could the outbreak have been prevented? The question has been argued inconclusively. But it seems to be established that the last of the British Viceroys, Lord Mountbatten, who prepared the partition, was warned by his advisers of the scale of the trouble which might be expected in the Punjab, and that he and his immediate staff underrated the advice. It is sad that the last months when Britain had responsibility in India were disfigured by this error of judgement and its appalling results.

The one consolatory fact was that the massacres did not spread further into India, as might easily have happened. In the Gangetic Plain there is a very large Moslem population, though it is a minority and could not have defended itself. For a time it was likely that the tales of the horrors in the Punjab would lead to the Hindus in India murdering a large part of these people. The cry could have gone up that the Moslems in India were a fifth column, plotting to rise and seize the government, enabling Pakistan to re-establish something like the old Moghul Empire. Great credit is due to the Indian government that, though in the shaken condition which went with partition and the transfer of power by the British, it was able to prevent the Punjab disaster from spreading.

The second crime of violence which shook India soon after independence was the assassination of Mr Gandhi in January 1948. He was killed by a Hindu who resented the restraint which he had placed on the communal war against the Moslems and who feared the effects of his influence upon Hindu orthodoxy. If the assassin had been a Moslem nothing could probably have restrained the Hindu fury against the many millions of Moslems still in India. Gandhi's death at the hands of his own people, though he was revered by the majority of them as none had been for centuries, was according to the pattern of the end of many of the great illuminators of mankind. His death removed a mentor from the government of the new Indian state, but may have prevented subsequent painful conflict between him and some of the more worldly Congress leaders.

These were the grim events of the early days of independence. But at once after these initial convulsions the new government gained prestige rapidly as it showed itself well able to carry on the administration of the country, maintain peace and security and at the same time to pilot the country through the social revolution needed to bring its archaic society into twentieth-century life – a task from which its predecessor had shrunk.

The government started with assets which proved of immense value and which helped to explain its success. One was the spirit of nationalism, which has proved to be the chief cement holding together the conflicting groups in the population. Another was the tradition of the rule of law and the desirability of national unity, all of which had grown up under the British Raj. Another was the civil service, the steel frame of India, which the Congress party, though formerly its critic, was much too intelligent to destroy.

Paradoxically another of the assets was the English language. This continued in use as the unifying official means of communication and the ordinary language of the middle class. It proved a strong power binding the country together; it was the very blood of the nationalist movement, for, without English, all-Indian nationalism might divide into a confusion of minor regional nationalisms. There was, of course, pressure from the xenophobes to abandon it, and gradually it will and should be superseded by indigenous languages. But most of the Congress leaders appreciated its function temporarily. For example, Mr Rajagopalachari, one of Gandhi's principal associates, in a speech at Madura University, said recently that the English language was the special gift to India of Saraswati, the Hindu goddess of learning.

'Our goddess Saraswati', he said, 'gave different languages to different peoples of the world. Why should we not claim what is our own? The English people came here, and for certain accidental reasons, causes and purposes they left behind a vast body of the English language. Why should we give them back this thing? The English are not entitled to it. It is ours. We need not send it to Britain along with Englishmen. It belonged to us by origin, the originator being Saraswati, and also by acquisition.'

Thanks in great measure to these assets, India in the first seven years of its independent life has been impressively stable. To maintain by constitutional means, and not by force, the government of its disparate society was a most remarkable achievement.*

Consider in more detail the record of the functioning of the parliaments. There is a parliament at the centre; there are the parliaments of the provinces. Parliamentary government is perhaps especially well suited to the Indian temperament. Indians like conversation. The parliaments have acted both decorously and constructively. Ministers have not overridden them; even a man with such a strong and rather intolerant will as Mr Nehru has shown himself a good parliament man; on their side, the parliaments have not gone in for barren obstruction. Of course the Indian parliaments have not functioned in quite the same way as those in the rest of the Commonwealth because the circumstances in India are in many ways different. For example, in the centre and in most of the provinces, there has been only one major party, the Congress, which, as the chief executive of the struggle against the British, had gathered into itself the most varied classes and interest groups. Thus in most of the assemblies there has been an overwhelmingly strong Congress party forming the government and a very weak opposition, and the struggle between parties which usually takes place on the floor of the parliament was in India transferred to struggles outside the parliament between different factions of Congress. Members of parliament have been perhaps rather too docile. They are less individualist than were the parliamentarians under the British Raj. Outstanding men are to-day less attracted to politics, or find it harder to get elected.

The high point of the parliamentary history of India was the general election in the mid-winter of 1951–2. This was carried out in perfect order and freedom, though the electorate had suddenly

* The maintenance of national unity was the more impressive because while under the British the government had been, until the closing years, a unitary one for all India, after independence it was on a federal basis. This might have accentuated the tendencies to division. But these were countered by the all-India unity of the Congress party, and the hold it had in almost all the provinces.

been increased from 30 million to 176 million, of which about 85 per cent were illiterate. The parties had to adopt visual symbols – such as an umbrella or a plough – to be placed on the ballot papers: the illiterate could then place their mark against the candidate of the party which they wished to support. The majority of voters never read a newspaper or hear the radio. In spite of these apparent handicaps the election was fought intelligently. All the evidence shows that the great mass of the simple people were somehow made aware of the basic issues, even if in a sketchy way, and that they weighed them seriously. Malpractices, intimidation, and bribery certainly took place: but they were less than was feared.

The general election was notable also because it brought into prominence for the first time the Indian Communist party. True, over most of the country it was still negligible. But in three of the southern provinces it won nearly the same number of seats as Congress. In the parliament at the centre, though it won only 27 seats compared with the 362 of Congress, it became the second largest party, thus obtaining the status of being the official opposition. Here was the shadow over the future. Here was the arrival of those who might eventually change the whole scene.*

That lay ahead. In the meanwhile the present was bright. After the election, and still more two or three years later, it could be said fairly that India had passed impressively its first tests. Its institutions commanded respect at home and abroad. Its prime minister, Nehru, had made himself one of the foremost figures in the world. It had a powerful army. Anxieties over possible famine, which as a post-war legacy beset the early years of independence, were being lessened. Industry, science, education were all in an active, creative condition. The political atmosphere was healthy. The government, while respecting the constitution, did not hesitate to promote constitutional changes where these were necessary. Thus the system showed flexibility and vitality. Opinion could be expressed more freely than perhaps in any other country of Asia. There was less fear among its citizens than elsewhere in Asia. Government was felt to be not too remote from most of the people, and it was responsive to them. Under Mr

* Indian Communism is discussed in detail below.

Nehru, the government, in the eyes of India, is not an aloof and unsympathetic 'they'. Concentration camps did not exist. At most times there were less than a thousand political prisoners.

There was, too, a sense of advance and of social purpose, and this is always of high importance in giving health to a society. Political power in the new India rests with the professional middle class, and this has inherited the ancient Hindu tradition of austere living. Its values are becoming dominant; the rich merchant or industrialist is not regarded with much respect. Government has not been operated merely in a routine manner. The large reforms of society which Congress had promised are under way. Some of them are relieving the tension in society. The extremes of wealth, for which India was once notorious, are already much reduced; a steeply progressive income tax is acting as a genuine equalizer of society. A part of Congress wishes to place a ceiling upon personal income. Land reform has been decreed and partly carried through. New enterprises have been created, social security widened, primary education extended, science adapted to the service of the country. By the Six Year Plan for economic development the government has hastened and controlled the general economic advance. Through all the various devices of administration, the new life is being promoted not only in the towns but also in the villages.*

* Perhaps the most imaginative act of the Indian government has been to organize the so-called community projects in the rural areas. These seem to have been invented by a remarkable American, Mr Mayer, who, during service in India in the war, travelled in the countryside; he reflected that if the idle labour of the peasants could be used, India would have found an instrument as effective as capital for transforming and modernizing its society. The system, which is controlled by provincial governments, is, in brief, to group every hundred villages as a unit, and to enquire from the villagers what constructive endeavours would most benefit them. Almost invariably the villagers ask first for water by means of tube wells, next for schools, and next for hospitals. Trained social workers then visit the villages, and explain the offer of the government that, if the villagers will contribute labour in the realization of their favourite project, the government will give other aid, in finance, materials, or technicians. Nearly a third of India is now covered with these projects. By 1961 all India will be covered. It is hard at present to say what results they are producing. But in some areas the success is quite evident; moreover an enthusiasm has developed among the

The exuberance of the new India is well expressed in a convocation address given recently at Calcutta by Sardar K. M. Panikkar. 'India is going through an immense process of regeneration. It has been my good fortune to travel over the length and breadth of India, to visit the less frequented areas of the country to see for myself what is happening. Nothing has gladdened my heart so much as the feeling I have received wherever I went that we were passing into a period of beneficient revolutionary changes brought about not by blood and thunder but the quiet and peaceful work of our people. Wherever you go, far south in Tinnevelly or Cape Comorin, or in the Himalayas, or in the arid plains of Rajasthan, you see great works in progress, immense undertakings, mighty transformations of land such as this country has never witnessed at any time before. I am not alluding merely to the gigantic projects, but to the programme in which thousands of villages, millions of people, are involved, which alter the outlook of the common man towards his surroundings and give him fresh hopes and new aspirations. It is a new and in many ways unfamiliar India which is being built up. It is changing not merely the face of our country but the character of our people. ... Let those who moan that free India is not building new temples which vie with Ellora, or constructing monuments which equal the Taj Mahal, remember that the transformation of life which is being attempted to-day, not merely in our irrigation scheme and in our new factories, but in the villages themselves, is creating a higher and greater civilization than we have ever enjoyed, a culture which is not confined to classes and groups but extends to the entire nation.'

Here is a Faust-like vision, of a whole nation achieving salvation through beneficient constructive activity – draining the marsh lands, reclaiming jungle, rearing great new cities. As long as the awareness continues that notable things are being done, and that India is in a phase of construction, India's health will be good. Yet there are also dark features. These too must be analysed.

peasants. The effects, if the system as a whole succeeds, is that the peasants no less than the townsmen in India will begin to see a visible material improvement, and this should help to prevent the farmers from being lured by Communist appeals.

THE weakness of the new India is that its political institutions, and also many of its social institutions, are copied from those of the sophisticated industrial society in the West. They form a thin crust upon the top of a society which consists chiefly of peasants who understand the new institutions hazily, and have little emotional attachment to them. The institutions are those of a middle class civilization. But the great majority of the Indian population are illiterate and poverty-stricken. They live in a Hindu tradition, which is partly archaic. This either prevents change, or else, by the frustrations it causes, provokes those who desire reform to take to violent courses rather than to constitutional ones.

The liberal and promising India of our day may fulfil the hopes which it has roused. But it is at least possible that it may turn in other directions – to an authoritarianism and cult of the Hindu tradition, or to Communism.

Those who believe that the wave of the future must carry Communism irresistably over all Asia see in India the conditions which may make Communist revolution fairly easy to bring about. Behind the facade of the constitutional institutions, the intelligentsia can work upon the poverty and despair of the masses; and the intelligentsia itself may be inclined towards Communism because it is too large a class, and because not enough jobs are open to it.*

The successes of the Communists at the general election of 1952 caused serious attention to be given to the origins and history of the Indian Communist party. Since Communists are conspiratorial, their records are usually scanty or secret, and are often destroyed. It is fortunate that the history of the party in India has been diligently studied while the material about it is still easy to come by. Mr Masani's book *The Communist Party of India* will prove useful for all future historians.

The party in India was founded in 1925, chiefly by British Communists. At first the main recruits were the intelligentsia, in

* About 15 per cent of each year's university graduates remain unemployed.

many cases the sons and daughters of leading civil servants and business men. The Party claimed the whole lives of its members, and provided them with quarters for communal living and rules of almost monastic austerity. It offered a clear-cut intellectual interpretation of the trends of the world, and this appealed to the logical mind of many Indians. For Chinese, with their language which lends itself to a vagueness of concept, the intellectual appeal of Communism had been less, and presumably was replaced by appeal to instinct and emotions.

During the war the Communists suffered a bad set-back because, under instructions from Russia, they supported the war effort at the time when Congress was in open rebellion against it. Thus for the true nationalist, Communism was marked down as the enemy of the nationalist cause, and as acting in the interests of powers outside India. The harm which it suffered it is hard to overstate. Except for this, Communism might have made rapid progress in the post-war years.

The perseverance and energy of the Communist leaders slowly repaired the damage. Advantage was taken of every disorder and of every grievance. In Hyderabad there had been temporary chaos because of the quarrel between the Nizam's government and Delhi; the Communists therefore concentrated great effort upon it, and in two of the districts where the administration had temporarily broken down they managed for a time to maintain something like a shadow government. In Madras they exploited the grievances of the Telugu speakers who wanted to form a separate linguistic province (which was later conceded to them by Congress). In Travancore-Cochin, where there was the highest rate of literacy in India combined with terrible poverty and unemployment, the conditions were made for them. It was in areas with such special circumstances that the Communists prospered in the general election. But they did not succeed in all the places where the conditions might have been expected to help them. Surprisingly they failed to win the industrial proletariat in the great cities such as Calcutta.

The general election of 1952 showed that the main mass backing for Communism came from the peasantry and the lower middle class; and lookers on, studying the results, asked uneasily a number of questions. Would the Communists be able to make out of this backing a mass support for the seizure of power? Would their appeal grow as they had longer time to organize propaganda? Would they be able to seduce more of the intelligentsia? What would be the outcome of the idealogical battle being fought in the middle class between the old-fashioned who were satisfied with the liberal ideals of parliamentarianism and individual liberty and those who thought that authoritarian Communism alone could carry out the social reforms which India demanded? Would the Communists be able to represent themselves ultimately as truer nationalists than Congress and thus steal from Congress the nationalist fervour? Would Congress eventually go the way of the Kuomintang? All these questions were anxiously asked when the Communist threat first began to be taken seriously as the result of the general election.

That was three years ago. It has become clear since then that the advance of Communism has slowed down, and in some places has changed to retreat. In recent provincial elections in Andhra they suffered badly. The forces of conservatism are still strong. The impression which India gives to the visitor is of a return to stability. The phase of upheaval seems to be over. Congress, has seemed to the voter to be doing well enough not to have forfeited its claims for support. A period soon after independence when in many provinces Congress became notoriously corrupt and inert has ended, and recently, partly because of Mr Nehru's urging, it has taken on new vigour. It may reform moderately and gently, but it does reform, and the pace is congenial to India. Thus Communism is blocked. Because of this frustration, the Communist leaders have been divided by faction.

The danger of Communism may therefore not look immediately serious. Yet the more patient Communist leaders are probably not despondent. If the greatest impediments to them are the prestige of Mr Nehru and the success of Congress, Mr Nehru is a mortal man, and who knows what will happen to Congress after he ceases to lead it? If it moved to the right, if it lost its present very sensitive contact with public opinion, it might rapidly lose its strength. As India becomes industrialized, the town proletariat will grow; and it is a fact of history that the discontent of a proletariat often increases with its growing prosperity. But the great hope of the Communists must continue to be the propulsive force of the peasantry, and of sixty million untouchables still suffering from monstrous social injustices in spite of all the assertions that their wrongs are being dealt with. One of the sombre facts about India to-day is that in spite of all the efforts of reform the standard of living of the peasant has fallen or at best is now remaining just constant. This happens because the population is increasing at the rate of five million a year. Perhaps science will find new ways of feeding them. But it is rational to be afraid of the outcome. The convulsions in China during the century were in part the result of a population crisis. India may not be spared.*

One of Gandhi's former disciples, Vinoba Bhave, has had perhaps the clearest vision of the dangers which might befall India from a hungry and desperate peasantry.† He is one of the dramatic figures of contemporary India. Like a prophet from the Old Testament he has been preaching the woe which is to come

* Some shrewd observations about the possibilities of Communism in India have been made by a former English Communist, Philip Spratt, who had an adventurous career in organizing the Indian Communist Party in its earliest days, and afterwards recanted. In his book *Blowing Up India*, he writes: 'India is a backward country – more so than Russia in 1917. Communism here would inevitably bring purges, genocide, massacres of scores of millions, whole provinces starved into submission, all the ideas of the past and all dissident ideas of the present stamped out with merciless rigour, systematic indoctrination of the whole people with patent falsehoods, universal espionage penetrating into every home, children denouncing their parents and publicly rejoicing at their execution. . . . Yet most people in India discuss this not very remote prospect with cool detachment.' Spratt thinks that this strange tolerance by India of the prospects of Communism is partly due to a special trait of the Hindu mind. Hindus, he says, assess conduct, not by the results which it produces but by the motive. Many of the Indian Communists are obviously young men with high idealism and willingness to sacrifice themselves. So it is widely accepted that there must be some merit in their actions, even if cool intelligence suggests that these actions may result in suffering on a prodigious scale.

† The danger of revolutionary feeling comes not so much from the poor small-holder or tenant farmer but from the landless labourer. Only recently has it been realized what a high proportion of Indian farmers cultivate no land at all, whether as owners or tenants.

unless the classes which own property take steps to forestall the peasants' grievances. He urges the landlords to assuage the land-hunger by shedding part of their holdings voluntarily and giving them to the landless, and he urges the townsmen similarly to give a portion of their capital to the poor. It is hard to think that such an ingenuous appeal would affect practical politics in any other country. But in India, Vinoba Bhave's personality and his warnings have awed landlords into giving four million acres in four years.* Of course these gifts are not large enough to change rural society, nor could gifts on a very much larger scale do this. But the interest taken in the movement shows how widely Communism is feared.

Communism may be helped by the rather dismal failure of the Indian socialists to establish a mass party which would oppose Congress but at the same time oppose totalitarianism. The Socialist party has many intellectually able leaders but they have failed to discover how to win votes or fight elections.† With each election their hopes and prestige fall, and the younger generation is thus discouraged from joining them.

Communism is not the only alternative or threat in India to liberalism. There is the rival, though less immediately conspicuous, danger of a kind of Hindu fascism. As the years pass, the classes which may become the chief repository of power are what might loosely be termed the lower middle class – clerks, foremen, shop-keepers, minor landlords, village merchants, minor technicians. Demagogues might see an opportunity of appealing for their support as the basis of a government directed essentially to maintaining existing economic rights and the traditional Hindu institutions – to preserve caste, to safeguard the joint family, to perpetuate the respect for cows and brahmins, to maintain the

---

* Some of the land given is inferior or useless. Some has been taken back from the poor as soon as Vinoba Bhave's back is turned. But the figure is nevertheless striking. There are delays over the distribution of donated land to the poor. The system for this needs improving.

† There is something very wrong with their election strategy. At the general election they won twice as many votes as the Communists but only half as many seats. The occasional high poll for them shows that they are not yet beyond hope, but they have still to become a true force in Indian politics.

suppression of the untouchables. Such a government would probably also be excessively chauvinist. It is true that while Jawaharlal Nehru is alive, a development of this kind is not very likely. One of the peculiarities of India is the influence which single dominant figures may exercise. After Gandhi, it is Nehru; and he is probably capable of preventing a swing by the country towards narrowness and reaction. But Nehru cannot survive for ever. Bagehot said that one of the peculiar qualities of the office of prime minister in Britain was that its holder could by his personality elevate the whole moral tone of his country's politics. Mr Nehru has done that in India. But what comes afterwards?*

One of the uncertainties rises because Indian society is changing so fast. It is hard to foresee what kind of man the Indian citizen will be a generation hence. Illiterate India may presently become literate; according to the government's plan, education will be universal by 1966. Will the newly educated Indian be more radical or more conservative? Who can say? Still only the top layer is politically active. When the whole mass stirs, who can tell what may happen?

The principal threat for the future lies in India's past – the past of arbitrary government and of convulsive violence which once was the main characteristic of the politics of the country, and which may reassert itself. The testing time will come when the sense of purpose falters, and when the leadership no longer speaks the mind of most of the country. The present age will be a celebrated one in Indian history, but there can be no illusion of its permanence. The fires of violence have flared too often. What do the rights of man amount to in a society where nature may sweep away millions in famine, pestilence, and catastrophe? The organization of the modern state is a thin crust. If it is broken, terrible eruptions may occur.

India is a country where a sense of security can be misleading. 'India is at present quiet,' said a Victorian Viceroy, 'as quiet as gunpowder.'

* Paradoxically, the Communists and the extreme Hindu organizations often collaborate in local action. This recalls the occasional joint action of Nazis and Communists in Germany when both were against the Weimar republic.

THE record in Pakistan has been rather less impressive than in India. But this was to be expected because the circumstances of the country have been less favourable for the smooth working of a liberal form of government. Pakistan consisted of those parts of the Indian sub-continent which for various reasons had been behindhand in developing the new institutions, new social classes, and industry which the contact with the West had brought into being.* Thus when Pakistan was created, it had a smaller middle class than India; and it was on the shoulders of the middle class that constitutional government had at first to be carried. Immediately after the creation of the state the middle class was weakened still further because a part of it was Hindu, and in West Pakistan (though not in the East) this part migrated almost entire to India.

Thus in Pakistan there was less awareness than in India about the nature of the liberal experiment which was being made, less sense of urgency that it should succeed, less emotional attachment to the new institutions and less understanding about how they ought to work. Since the middle class was so much smaller, there were fewer educated men, fewer trained civil servants, fewer sophisticated politicians. These were more conscious than in India of an unsympathetic or hostile background – the society of an illiterate peasantry and of obscurantist mullahs. Throughout the eight years of Pakistan history, the mullah has been a threat to government and tranquillity in a way that the Hindu fanatic has not been in India.

These disabilities have been reflected in the political history. Unlike India, Pakistan found much difficulty in voting itself a constitution. At the time of emancipation and partition, the former parliament of undivided India was separated in two, one for India and one for Pakistan. As constituent assemblies they

---

* Partly this was because the Moslems, who had governed India before the British, had at first guarded themselves against Western influence, while the Hindus had on the contrary set out to modernize their society as the best way of restoring Hindu authority.

were expected to produce the constitutions of the new countries. The Indian assembly finished its work rapidly; the Pakistan assembly took seven years, and as it had lost touch with its constituents, who regarded its continued existence as a scandal, it was finally dissolved by the Governor-General. Its members had procrastinated, not because of the difficulties of constitution making, but because the enjoyment of their emoluments seemed more attractive than exposing themselves to the hazards of making a career under the new constitution they were supposed to be producing.

While the assembly had been in existence, Pakistan history had not been smooth. Mr Jinnah, the great founder of the state, died very early – within seven months of Gandhi – exhausted by his efforts. His successor, Liaquat Ali Khan, was assassinated. Liaquat's successor, Nazim-ud-din, was dismissed by the Governor-General in circumstances which, though there was no actual breach of law, were hardly in the spirit of constitutional government.* The Moslem League, the party by whose efforts the state had been created, lost its authority and its mass support. There was economic crisis in the time of falling prices after the Korean war. There was a mysterious conspiracy against the government in the army. There were dangerous riots in the Punjab, organized by mullahs who thought the government not sufficiently obscurantist. East Bengal, the eastern part of the state – which contains a majority of the population and pays more than half the revenue – became increasingly hostile to the western half and to the central government. In a general election in East Bengal, the Moslem League was swept away. The cabinet which succeeded it talked so openly of secession that the central government stepped in and suspended its newly-elected legislature and government.

Consider, however, the brighter side of the record. The wonder in Pakistan is not that it has met so many difficulties, as that it has overcome so many. Because of the circumstances in which the state came into being, its government lacked at first much

* Pakistan has been dependent on its great men. Without Jinnah it would not have existed. Without Liaquat Ali Khan it would probably have foundered. Ghulam Mohammed (who retired this year from the office of Govenor-General) gave it a new lease of life.

of the ordinary material machinery of administration, and had to deal with a flood of problems which might have overturned men of less determination.* Nationalism and the impetus of the new state carried them through. Law and order were maintained. A host of refugees from India were settled. As conditions became normal, government maintained its authority with noticeable mildness. There were few political prisoners. The press was in substance free, though there were a few foolish persecutions of journalists.

In 1955, though the future of Pakistan seemed less certain than India's, it was irrational to be pessimistic. The threat of Communism had hardly begun to be serious. Islam, which is a movement of social discipline, makes society relatively easy to organize. The main shadow which lies over the country is that, since it is a Moslem country with many features similar to the Moslem countries of the Middle East, it may move like them towards dictatorship. The follies of the politicians may push the cabinet and civil service towards this, even if they wished nothing less. A recent crisis over the dissolution of the constituent assembly showed how this might happen. But if there is moderation, it may be prevented.

23   SOUTH-EAST ASIA

BESIDES India and Pakistan there were two other successor states to the British Empire in Asia – Burma and Ceylon. There was Malaya, destined to become a successor state. There were the successor states of the other Western empires – the Philippines, Indo-China, Indonesia. There was also Siam, which, though it had never been a part of a Western empire, and therefore was in no sense a successor state, had been under Western influence. All these lands form the troubled area of South-east Asia – the Asian Balkans.

* The foreign office in Pakistan had to be set up on a budget of only £10,000, extracted by rather irregular means from Indian revenues.

Since 1947 the theme in nearly all these countries has been the same. It was the attempt to operate a democratic system copied from the home governments of the former imperial powers; there was no attempt after emancipation to return to the former monarchical institutions of the pre-Western days. But the theme's development was less satisfactory than in India. In Indonesia, in Indo-China, in Burma, in the Philippines and Malaya there was confusion, widespread fighting, and disillusion. After seven years some of the countries, it is true, have overcome what seemed to be the most threatening dangers; but none has the stable, promising look of India.

Their tribulations were not really surprising. Except for the Philippines, they had not enjoyed the same careful preparation for self-government as India; at least the preparation had not lasted so long. Their societies had not evolved slowly and ripened and become self-confident, like that of India, able to manage itself when the Western imperialist was ousted. A thriving and competent middle class had not come into being, since commerce in most of the countries of the region was monopolized by Westerners or Chinese. Only a few of the local peoples had been admitted to the upper reaches of the administrative services.

These countries would, therefore, even in the most favourable circumstances have appeared rather shaky. And circumstances were not favourable. The recent war and Japanese invasions, though they probably very much hastened the end of the old empires, had also caused upheaval and change which brought general violence, weakened the old moral restraints, and spread everywhere the sense of uncertainty and the habit of disobedience to government. A great many of the arms laid down by the Japanese at their surrender passed into private ownership. Conditions were ideal for the turbulent. Among the many minority groups, fear increased that they would be outrageously oppressed by the new national governments, and the instinct was to forestall this by rebelling first.

It was surprising that some of the governments managed as well as they have done. Ceylon has fared best, but Ceylon started with the most advantages. Burma, where for a time government almost ceased as the result of civil war – a complex war between

144

the government and minority people the Karens, and also between the government and two rival bands of Communists – has in the last three years recovered remarkably. To-day it has a cabinet which is obeyed but which is responsive to a parliament elected by tolerably free elections. The Philippines, which copied the American rather than the Western form of democracy, have elected a reforming president, under whom government is carried on constitutionally but effectively. A formidable guerilla movement of the Communists, or near Communists, the Huks, has been broken.

The calamity in other parts of the region is that the effort at building up the new governments became entangled with a wasting and anachronistic struggle between nationalism and the former imperial overlords. In Indonesia and Indo-China, the imperialist system, though its day was obviously over, was not ended quickly and neatly, as it had been in India and Burma. The Dutch and French after the expulsion of Japan tried at first to restore their former authority; and when it was clear that this was beyond their strength, tried to hand over their power to a moderate section of nationalists from whom they could get better terms for their interests, economic and political, than from the extremists. The confusion which resulted, the divisions among the nationalists, and the obstacles to the restoration of normally efficient administration proved the wisdom of those who had carried out the abrupt British withdrawal from India. In a war between nationalism and a moribund imperialism, power on the nationalist side passes into the hands of the most radical.

Indonesia was free by 1950. Its history since then has been rather disappointing. Corruption and inefficiency have been bad. Only this year has the government risked the holding of general elections. Perhaps, in any case, Indonesia's course would have been full of troubles because of its social structure and past. But the circumstances of its emancipation increased the troubles. In Indo-China the struggle lasted much longer, brought the world near to war, and delivered part of Indo-China into the hands of the Communists, with the rest perhaps to follow later. France's failure in its policy in Indo-China was dismal. For a short time in 1946 it had seemed that France would come to terms with the

Annamite leader Ho Chi Minh as Britain had done with Gandhi. But it missed its chance, partly because the rapid changes of government in France did not permit France to have a consistent colonial policy. Moreover in Indo-China, as in other French colonies, there existed a very large number of Frenchmen of more or less humble position who held the lesser posts in the technical services which in India were as a matter of course left to the people of the country. This large class in Indo-China – the ' colons ' – has strong support in the French parliament, and had a continuously reactionary influence upon French policy. France became trapped in a war with the Annamite nationalists which drew to Indo-China such large forces that France's influence in Europe was at vital moments paralysed. The losses in action among young French officers was for some years larger than the output of new officers from the French military academies. Even the panache of the exploits of Marshal de Lattre de Tassigny did not give to the war an appeal which could catch the imagination; and it ended squalidly at the seige of Dienbienphu. In the meanwhile the nationalists against whom the French had fought had turned into avowed Communists and were allies of China; and the rival nationalists whom the French had tried to turn into allies were regarded in most of Indo-China as traitors to the national cause.

The final settlement in Indo-China is not yet decided. The long struggle drew in the external great powers, America and China, which though not in actual combat over Indo-China, are backing one side or the other. Thus South-east Asia has come to play the traditional part of a Balkans in attracting the rivalry of the great powers. Its significance has ceased to be simply its domestic affairs, interesting though these may be, but their effect upon world politics.

In the British colony of Malaya the pattern has been different. Here also at the end of the war Britain, the imperial power, did not hand over power; but this was because, unlike the circumstances in Indo-China and Indonesia, there was no clear-cut national party to challenge the return of British authority, and no party which would have been capable at the time of carrying on the government. Unlike the other countries, Malaya is divided fairly evenly between two communities, the Malays and the

Chinese. At the end of the war, Malay nationalism was only in its start; and most Chinese nationalists were more interested in maintaining their economic advantages than in gaining political power; it was remarked cynically that as long as they could milk the colony they did not want the responsibility of owning it also. In spite of this, Britain had recognized, at least in principle, that the winding up of its rule must happen sooner or later; and it was ready to begin the advance to self-government by stages, on similar lines to what had happened in India.

The Communist rebellion, which started in 1948, caused many complications, but certainly speeded up the evolution of self-government. It has been a great forcing house of politics. It compelled people to be interested in politics when before they had been content to be indifferent. The moves by the government in organizing the people to co-operate against Communists were moves which prepared them for acting politically as a modern country.

The rebellion was made almost entirely by Chinese, not Malays. And it was a rising of only a small minority of the two and a half million Chinese; it seems that at no time were there more than 5,000 guerillas in action. Because of this it was logically correct to say that it was the movement of a small minority and was not a national uprising. But it was a rebellion which could not be put down. Full-scale war on the communist gangs with the use of the most modern weapons, heavy army reinforcements from Britain, a great enlargement of the police, reforms of the administration, social reforms – all failed to end the insurrection. The Communists were driven from time to time to change their tactics, to lie low, to hide passively in the depths of the jungle. But their organization remained intact. Not a single member of the Politburo was killed or surrendered. It became clear that even if the rebellion had flagged, it could be revived at any time with ease. New instructions from outside, a shipload of arms, the arrival of new agitators or leaders. could start it off again. Moreover the centre of activity might move at any time from the jungle to the cities – to the workers and students – where it might be even more formidable. The mass of the Chinese population understood this as well as the more perceptive British officials, and were resolved to ensure their future by giving partial co-operation to the Communists. Again and again the British army said that if it were assured of the aid of the civilian population it could put down the rebellion completely; by cajolery and discipline the aid was sought, but, though it might be given sporadically, it was never whole-hearted. The Communists could rely on hidden collaborators for supplies and money.

Fortunately the British Government, taking stock of the lesson of Indo-China, seems to have decided that the best hope of avoiding being entrapped, as the French were entrapped, is to press on with the setting up of a national government in Malaya, and also in Singapore, the great port which forms rather artificially a separate entity. To those successors it will bequeath the task of fighting the Communists, and, with the departure of the British, the Communists will no longer be able to claim that they are leading the country in a war against imperialism. The national movement was spurred on by Britain itself. After a slow start it is gathering momentum. Elections have been held in both Malaya and Singapore; a part of their governments are now formed by elected ministers. With these changes have come riots and upheaval, at least in Singapore. To some of the British on the spot, the pace may now seem too hot. In Singapore especially there is going to be continual trouble with the Chinese students, who are excellently organized, energetic, willing to sacrifice themselves, and for the most part more attracted by China than by the idea of an independent political life. There is bound to be collision with them. But from now on British policy in Malaya will be a race against disaster – a race to build up the institutions to be the inheritors of British power before Britain is engulfed militarily.

The British task in Malaya is complicated because of the divisions between the Malay and Chinese peoples. They have to be welded together as part of the process of a British departure. It is a welding, not a merging. The Malays and Chinese – and the Indians who form a large minority – cannot become a single people. The task is to create an atmosphere in which different and distinct peoples will collaborate with give and take in working democratic institutions – in which the Chinese think of themselves as belonging to Malaya, and do not act on behalf of China.

Siam, the remaining country of the region, has had a different history because it was never a colony; and it is not seriously attempting to run a democratic or liberal form of government. Of course it has been much influenced by its very close contacts with the West. But it preserved its monarchy; and its revolution, which broke the monarchical absolutism in 1932, did little more than admit new classes into the government, which previously had been a monopoly of the very numerous relatives of the royal family. Since then its system has been a curious and rather slovenly and corrupt bureaucracy, controlled by the army and police (with the navy occasionally protesting). Excesses of arbitrariness are prevented by tradition and also by the incompetence of the government machine. There is little discontent. Compared with other Asian countries, Siam is economically well off, and this has helped to exclude tension. By the standards of the rest of Asia, the people are extraordinarily unfevered and uninterested in politics; even the students do not demonstrate.* Degree, priority, and place dominate nearly everybody's social and political thought and behaviour. Siamese society is a pyramid, and the units are content to remain within their place. The main danger to the state comes, not from restiveness of the Siamese people, but from the very large Chinese minority. Siam cannot remain unaffected by the world around it. But in the past it has had a knack for evading storms and upheavals. It may continue to do so.

A common feature of the governments in most of the countries of South-east Asia is the youth of the politicians. The seizure of power after the war was a young men's movement. The old were brushed aside; and the young who removed them have not yet become old. Here is a contrast to India and Japan; here may be a link with China though the principal Chinese leaders are ageing; and here also may be an explanation of some of the excessive enthusiasm of some of the governments of the region.

* Students at the principal university make remarks unthinkable elsewhere in Asia. 'I do not believe that anyone in this world has ever been driven to crime or died of hunger,' said one; and another, 'I suppose that, if every country had a real king, the danger of war would be infinitely less.'

PART FOUR

The Rest of Asia

24 JAPAN

WHAT in the meanwhile had happened to the other Far East country, Japan? Historically the similarities of China and Japan have often been close, and events in one deeply affect the other. Revolution in China was bound ultimately to shake Japan to the core. But in the first period of the Chinese revolution Japan was protected because it was still under American military occupation.

The post-war occupation of Japan by the United States had been one of the curious episodes of modern history. In the previous hundred years Japan had been the one Asian country which had kept upon fairly level terms with the West. Though it had undergone radical changes because of the Western impact, these changes had the appearance of being decided by the Japanese themselves. The old Japanese conviction of their invincibility was reinforced. Then right at the end of the period of Western ascendancy, Japan experienced the fate endured already by most of the rest of Asia. Because it lost its war-time gamble, it lay at the mercy of its conqueror more completely, whether to be conserved or reshaped, than China, in the previous half century its despised rival, had ever been. For a few years America enjoyed the power of being in Japan the undisputed political architect which Britain had had in India in the mid-nineteenth century.

The Japanese leaders who, risking the anger of the army officers and the fanatics, carried the country through to the surrender, were ready and even glad to see some of the reforming measures of the United States. The military and the patriotic gangs had grown uncontrollable by any government in Japan.

Their elimination caused relief. The restoration of parliament, the revival of parties, the fostering of a free press were received calmly. They gave Japan a third chance; in the eighties of the last century and the twenties of this it had wished to turn liberal. A fanatical minority of the people had been able to prevent it; that had been a tragedy for other countries besides Japan. There was no chagrin at seeing this minority at last in its turn thwarted. Moreover, in the shock of defeat the mood of nearly the whole country had changed. For a hundred years Japan's history has been one of oscillation, of restless empirical experimentation. When it was found that its military ambitions had led it to disaster, Japan was prepared to drop them abruptly and follow other courses. A large part of the people became pacifist. They were thankful that the military adventure was over, even though they had not opposed it. They followed the line common with nations in defeat; there was a new stress on individualism and on interest in new philosophies; all this was similar to what happened in Germany after 1945.

Probably the Japanese leaders in the capitulation had comforted themselves that reforms which went too far and which threatened the heart of Japanese civilization would meet with a national resistance which would be insuperable. The Japanese imagination, perhaps because of the small Japanese stature, has always been obsessed with ideas of how the weaker may overcome the stronger. The Japanese relied upon the national cult of judo or jujitsu to save the essential Japanese traditions. But what were these? The trouble in Japan is that, while the country is strongly aware of its civilization, it is peculiarly difficult to define in clear terms what are its desirable and indispensable features, and much of the anxious thought among Japanese intellectuals is to decide what constitutes Japanese civilization essentially.*

Resistance to change was aided by circumstances. One of the

---

* As happens so often in an occupied country, the inhabitants began to be more conscious than before of their difference from their occupiers. Japanese, in order to distinguish themselves from Americans, began to cultivate strenuously the traditional Japanese attitudes. This may have helped to stimulate the making of Japanese films, Japan's most striking post-war achievement culturally.

misfortunes of the American occupation of Japan was that it appeared grotesque. Nearly everybody who saw it in operation saw at once its ludicrous side. A very large force of administrators and technical experts, dressed in army uniform, were brought into the country, and, without knowing the language, started, each in his corner, trying to build up new Japanese institutions which would look like American institutions, and trying to make Japanese laws into American laws. This huge corps re-enacted in Tokio and Japanese provincial cities the life of Washington, and hardly came into touch with the Japanese.* To create such an occupation force, so aloof, so busy, so well provided for, was a remarkable achievement of organization. In its strange features, in its methods of work, and in its results the occupation force resembled that in Germany. But the people occupied kept their thoughts to themselves more than the Germans, and were probably more puzzled.

The Americans disarmed Japan completely. They insisted on a land reform – less radical than is sometimes supposed. They broke up the great monopoly firms. They fostered trade unions. They barred from public life a large section of the public men, including Mr Hatoyama, the present prime minister. They gaoled those who had played a sinister part in the war, including Mr Shigemitsu, the present foreign minister. They took away the control of the local police from the central government. They reformed the schools. They rewrote the constitution.

One of the most revered institutions, the Emperor, they did not touch. Whether to spare the Emperor had been anxiously debated. It was decided that, as he was ready to co-operate, and as he had played a decisive and courageous part in bringing about the surrender, he should be allowed to continue. It was argued that if he was seen to favour submission, most of the country would also submit. But he was to cease to be half divine, and was to become the constitutional head of the state. This was formally proclaimed in the new constitution.

The decision not to remove the Emperor, which may have been

* The Americans abolished old street names, and renamed the streets with letters and numbers, as in Washington. The Japanese simply ignored this.

very justifiable, decided the total result of the American occupation. It was accepted as the token that there was to be no social revolution, and the conservative forces regained confidence. Their skilful resistance to innovation became more effective. The Japanese praised America, expressed their gratitude for the mildness of the occupation, showed interest in all the new plans – genuine interest for the Japanese have always had a passion for novelty – and silently and effectively thwarted all they disliked. Perhaps they did not get as much amusement out of the comic situation as they might have done, for the Japanese have little humour.

The occupation lasted for seven years, during which America spent vast sums upon maintaining and reviving the Japanese economy. During this time the world had changed. America's chosen ally in Asia, China, had repudiated its part.

America therefore needed a substitute ally in Asia. India it mistrusted; it fell back on Japan, which it had reformed, and which was professing to remake itself in America's image. For America it was a return to an old friendship, for at the beginning of the century America had felt warm feelings for Japan, and sympathized with it against Tsarist Russia; its feelings only cooled when Japan became too strong and independent. By 1951 America was ready to do all in its power to set Japan again upon its feet. By the treaty of San Francisco – made in September of that year – Japanese sovereignty was restored. Simultaneously Japan became an ally of America.

A part of what the occupation had brought about had then to be undone, with the approval or at the instigation of the United States, whose main desires was to see the emergence of a Japan which was stable, non-Communist, and strong enough to take its part in containing Communism. Most of those who had been disqualified from politics came back into the arena. Some took high posts. The cartels re-formed. The police was again placed under central control. The revival of the army began, though in the teeth of the sentiment of the greater part of the Japanese people, who had become very anti-militarist. But if the trend was conservative, it was still a fairly respectable conservatism. The gangster patriotic groups were kept down. Japan developed as the better elements in Japan might have desired it to do before the war.

The occupation had begun with America feeling horror towards Japanese civilization in all its branches; it ended with America expressing admiration. Nor was the admiration altogether misplaced. For although Japan had behaved so ill in the thirties, yet Japan, next to India, had come nearest to making a success of democratic institutions and to respecting the rights of its citizens. For brief periods the Diet had worked as a parliament genuinely controlling the executive. By virtue of having been in existence for a long time, it had taken roots. It had become part of the landscape; Japanese were willing to work through it. Through Japan's defeat in war, the reaction which had nearly overthrown the liberal – or quasi-liberal – system was checked, and Japan became again one of the few functioning centres of liberalism in Asia.

The cause of liberalism might thus be served by Japan playing a larger part in the world. In the immediate post-war period this seemed unlikely. It appeared that Japan had fallen, not to rise again; it had owed its period of glory to the weakness of China, and this was over. Its geographical situation rendered it terribly insecure. But in the middle fifties, there are signs of a new turn. Alone among the Asian countries, it possesses the scientific skill to make large-scale use of atomic power. If there should be some years of peace, and influence should be decided by economic vitality as much as by military force, Japan's part in world affairs may grow.

Yet it must not be thought that Japan is now a stable country, with its problems solved, or that its attachment to the liberal ideal will now be steadfast.

Japan, in its revival, has conserved a society which in some respects lends itself easily to Communism. The discipline of the people has continued. This discipline had enabled them to preserve so much under defeat and occupation; but, given a change in the direction at the top, the discipline might as easily be linked with Communism as with the traditional form of society. The society is divided between a large proletariat and a very small class of capitalists; the middle class continues to be small. This was the type of society in Tsarist Russia which had facilitated the Bolshevik revolution. The student class, very poor and finding it desperately hard to get employment, may be attracted by any

154

system which promises secure jobs. Even the army might be attracted. Before the war, it had opposed liberal ideas, but had been attracted by extremism in all forms, of the left as well as of the right. When the army is recreated in Japan, it cannot be taken for granted that it will oppose Communism by instinct. Another important circumstance is that Japan, volatile in its interests and attachment, is once again developing an extraordinary regard for China. While public opinion in Japan is extremely hostile to Russia, it is fascinated by China. In the past it has taken most of its civilization from China; for fifty years it presumed to disdain it; but after Japan's own defeat and with the growing prestige of the Communists at Peking, Japan has reverted to its earlier attitude. Its attachment to China is perhaps the most constant thing in all Japanese history.

All these facts may encourage the Communist powers in hoping that Japan will eventually be included in their fold. And other circumstances may make them more optimistic, especially Japan's economic position. Over-populated, it depends for life upon its industrial export. Its territorial losses after the war deprived it of both raw materials and markets. A recession in international trade can bring crisis very swiftly, as it does in Britain also. The population is still increasing, even though the birth rate is falling slightly, and it is hard to see how it can be provided for when it has passed the 100 million, which is expected to happen by 1970. All these stresses and strains make Japan appear a promising subject for the Communist powers anxious to subvert it; and they can take still more confidence from the fact that the natural economic and cultural links of Japan are to a great extent with China.*

An interesting feature of Japan since the war is that there has been no nationalist leader of note. This continues an old tradition. There had been no single outstanding leader of Japanese nationalism in the days when Japan was terrifying Asia. Japan has a peculiar aversion from spectacular leaders. None of them

* The Communist Party in Japan is trying at present to appeal to Japanese nationalism, and for the purpose is representing itself as not very radical. It is trying to infiltrate all organizations where it can gain a footing, and is advocating a united front of left-wing parties. This is a change from the militant policies at the time of the Korean war which lost it support.

survives for very long. Everything in public life in Japan is arranged by groups and factions, usually working in the shadows. To identify which are the principal ones at any given time is a main task in analysing Japanese affairs.

25

RUSSIAN ASIA

RUSSIAN ASIA is the part of Asia where in the years since 1947 Communism has been a going concern – where it has not been in process of coming into being or in the first stage of Communist triumph. Russian Asia has also been the part of the continent not agitated by a conflict between people becoming emancipated and foreign governments.

In Russian Asia since the end of the last war, the major trends and policies of the Russian government have continued, changing their emphasis and direction from time to time, but forming a pattern which can be clearly read.

In the long view, probably the major happening in the post-war period has been the strengthening of the control of the Great Russians upon Soviet Asia. The pretence that the Asian Communist republics are autonomous becomes less and less supportable. Migration from European Russia has continued the whole time, especially into Kazakhstan; thus the proportion of Central Asian people to the Great Russians is steadily, if slowly, falling.* Russian customs become more predominant. The cultural policies of the government in Moscow have been directed increasingly against local nationalism. In the first days of Communism there had been a genuine attempt to gratify the peoples of Central Asia by treating their local culture with an exaggerated respect, even while denying them political liberty. But from the end of the war, the policy of Moscow, though it has veered and shifted from time to time, has been to deplore too much local pride. Formerly the Russian Communists, to mark their detestation of colonialism, had approved of the Asian leaders who had

* The overall proportion of settlers to natives is not less than one to four, and is much greater in some areas.

stood up to Tsarist imperialism. Now the leaders who resisted Russia, whether Tsarist or Communist, are all condemnable, for it is assumed that Russia, even under the old régime, should have been recognized as the agent of progress in the confined circumstances cf the age. Russia was by nature the elder brother of the peoples of Central Asia, and not to have recognized this was blindness. The young men of Asia who were to win favour from Moscow had to devote themselves admiringly to the study of the Russian language, Russian history, and Russian culture. Perhaps the most remarkable and original act of the government has been systematically to russify the Turkic languages.

It is in administration that the dominance of the Great Russians shows most clearly. The U.S.S.R. has never been a genuine federation. In essential matters the whole union has been rigidly controlled from the centre. The centre may arbitrarily redraw the boundaries of one of the federal units or even abolish it altogether. Thus Moscow always maintained a comprehensive power of intervention in the affairs of the Asian republics. After the war it seems to have decided to extend its control still further. This was because of wartime experience; the Asian soldiers in the Russian army had shown themselves anything but dependable. They had often allowed themselves to be taken prisoner without much resistance, and out of the prisoners of war Germany had been able to recruit a force of about 180,000 – chiefly Turkic speakers – to change sides and fight against Russia. If they were unreliable in war, Moscow regarded them as no less uncertain in peace.

Russian government everywhere in Asia has maintained a facade of administrations manned by the people of the region, both in the Central Asian republics and in the Far East. But these administrations are strictly supervised, partly by the N.K.V.D., partly by the local organs of the Communist Party, and both of these are staffed chiefly by Great Russians. That the supervision is effective is shown by the purges and disappearances of ministers and high officials of the Asian governments. Any of these who began to appeal to local nationalist feeling, which obviously is still strong, would quickly be removed.

Thus the huge Russian empire in Asia is centrally directed. In all its vast area the picture is essentially the same. The power of the state is used, persistently and remorselessly, to create a new society, to transform steppe and tundra, to build modern cities, to industrialize, to break down old ways. Nomadism is practically eradicated; old tribal organization has been shattered. The women are out of purdah. Everywhere there is collectivization or full state ownership. Steadily the colonists from European Russia move into Asian territories. Everywhere literacy is increasing with great rapidity. Everywhere the new class of Soviet 'managerial man' is being created in the young administrators, scientists, doctors, veterinaries, engineers mass produced in the new schools and colleges. Everywhere humanity is treated as so much raw material out of which the Soviet Utopia is to be constructed. There are no inhibitions about moving a whole people across half a continent, or abruptly from the stone age into the machine age, if the needs of the Soviet plan require it.

An immense amount has perished – whole tribes, entire social classes such as the begs and khans who used to rule Central Asia. There has been genocide on a grand scale. If fond memories of the past remain, if there is still attachment to past history, national heroes, national folk-tales, nobody yet knows how long they will endure. If Moscow is still tolerant of Islam (in spite of fits and starts of a campaign directed against it) the mullahs have lost their power and exist on sufferance. Out of this destruction a new world has been created. It is a world full of schools, libraries, hospitals, veterinary centres, parks, theatres, circuses, roads. Probably most of the younger generation accept what has been done and look back upon the pre-revolutionary past with abhorrence. There is no doubt that Russia has succeeded in creating a new civilization in the part of Asia which it controls, though whether it is a good civilization, whether it is congenial to the human spirit, is a matter which only the future historian, surveying both the past and this present picture, will decide.* It is a civilization –

* Not all Russia's projects for development are succeeding. The raising of livestock in the Central Asian republics has not yet recovered from the slaughter of the herds which took place when the nomads were dragooned in the thirties. Some of the great irrigation projects in Turkestan, which were advertised as having been started, have faded altogether from the news. The inference is that they may be in difficulties, or have been abandoned.

a modernization – imposed by the Russians. It is not a new civilization evolved because of a vital national revival among the Turkic peoples.

As far as can be reasonably guessed, the changes brought about are irreversible. In Russian Asia the old world is broken, dead, and cannot be revived; the peoples subjected in the nineteenth century are not going to recover their freedom; and what happens within the territories lies – unless Russia is defeated in a war – within Russia's firm control.

The part of Central Asia outside Russia's control – Tibet and Sinkiang – also passed under the Communists, but the Chinese not the Russians. A withdrawal of its pressure from Sinkiang was part of the price which Russia paid for the Chinese alliance. Tibet was taken over by China by armed invasion in 1950. How the imperialism of Chinese Communism in Central Asia compares with Russian imperialism there is not yet enough information to say. In Tibet, China is moving slowly, and evidently at present hopes to use the Dalai Lama as its instrument. He has been taken to Peking and indoctrinated; so has his rival, the Panchen Lama. It may be that for the present Peking will allow Tibet – and some other border regions – considerable autonomy in all except military matters and foreign policy. But Sinkiang it is likely to bring under the full Communist system even though it has given it recently the status of an autonomous region instead of that of a province.

The consolidation of Russian and Chinese authority over all Central Asia has had one momentous consequence. It has ended the importance of nomad peoples as the makers of history. For many centuries the nomads had hung threateningly on the outskirts of the settled land empires. The Huns and the Mongols caused extreme devastation of civilized life. Nomad invasions were a main cause of the unhappy failures in northern India in evolving the political institutions; promising starts were interrupted. But to-day it seems most unlikely that nomad hordes will ever again be on the move. Much of the pasture land is being ploughed. The children of the nomads will presently be assimilated by the rival civilizations. One of the main historic ways of life is thus being ended in our time.

26 POVERTY

THE Asian continent in which the drama is being played is the poorest part of the world. Poverty is, of course, not evenly distributed; some countries are comparatively well off. But over vast and thickly inhabited territories the poverty is the grimmest to be found in the twentieth century. Life, whether for the peasant or for the urban worker, is a painful and endless struggle, the continuous wearisome expenditure of labour, in conditions usually of disease and squalor, in order to win a livelihood which at best is by Western standards miserable, and with the constant prospect that in spite of all exertions the adverse circumstances will prove too great – that there will be drought or flood or other natural calamity producing famine, or that a war will disrupt families and destroy villages and crops, or that the factories will close down and there will be starvation in the towns. Life in most of Asia is still grim and short.

Consider the state of affairs in India.

'Expressed in real terms,' said an article recently in the *Economist*,* 'India's poverty translates itself into inadequate incomes at every level. A science demonstrator in a university may get £2 a week; a schoolteacher in Orissa has to make do on 10s. The agricultural labourer earns in some states as little as 1s 10d a day, and nowhere, even at harvest, will he earn more than 4s or 4s 6d; and he only works perhaps 200 days a year. The cottage industry worker and the village artisan do little better. ... Only the worker in modern industry does reasonably well; an unskilled labourer in a good firm may get (including his dearness allowance and bonus)

* From *The Economist*, 22 January 1955.

£2 a week, a skilled worker £3 or more; but he quite often pays for his relatively high wage with impossibly bad housing. Clerks do no better. In government service they may begin at £1 a week and do well ever to rise above £3. . . . Small holdings, subsistence farming and a precarious dependence upon the monsoon mean pitilessly low incomes for all engaged in agriculture. Only 16 per cent of the countryside spend more than £200 a year; fully one-half of all families have less than £100, one-fifth have less than £50. In the great city of Bombay, India's wealthiest urban centre, only 50 per cent of the people have about £100 a year, only 8 per cent above £300.'

That is India. Parts of South-east Asia and China are still poorer.

There is lassitude because of under-nourishment. Villages and towns are often filthy and gimcrack. Social services are sketchy because there is not enough revenue to pay for them.* Poverty is a drag on political progress. It hampers education. It prevents the growth of a prosperous middle class. By provoking class hatred it weights the chances against the success of democratic institutions. Of course there is no certainty that economic improvement would bring about calmer politics; sometimes a moderate prosperity, freeing people from their absolute preoccupation with daily toil, helps on revolution. But poverty such as exists in many parts of Asia can very well serve the interests of Communism.

The poverty itself is not the only reason for alarm. The crucial fact is that in many Asian countries the poverty has been growing worse, at least until recently, and the gap between the standard of living in Western countries and Asia is growing wider. Often it is taken for granted that Asia must have shared, even if on a small scale, in the spectacular increase of the world's wealth during this century. But this is a mistake, even if there have been occasional booms. It is Asia's misfortune that most of the countries of the continent are not yet at the stage of development where they can take advantage of many of the new scientific discoveries, including the use of atomic power. (Japan is an exception.) Thus

* To take a single but striking example. A recent report by the ILO say that in Baluchistan – in Pakistan – there are 118,000 married women. But there are only 19 midwives.

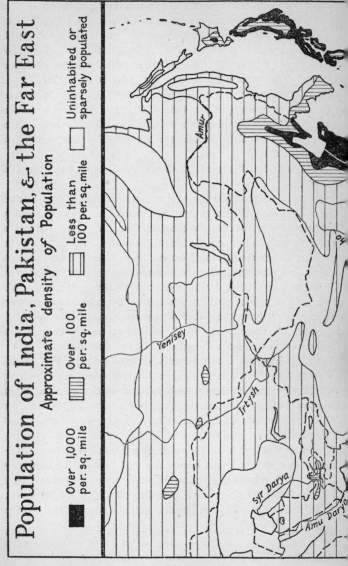

Population of India, Pakistan, & the Far East

Approximate density of Population

■ Over 1,000 per. sq. mile

▥ Over 100 per. sq. mile

▤ Less than 100 per. sq. mile

☐ Uninhabited or sparsely populated

its continuing poverty goes side by side with ever-growing wealth in the industrial countries. With the sharpening political awareness of Asia, it would be an excellent thing if the disparity were now to diminish. Instead it grows larger.

The most recent authoritative account of the economic circumstances in the continent is to be found in the Economic Survey of Asia and the Far East made by the United Nations for the year 1954. It showed that the situation was worse than it had been before the last war.

'Despite the considerable effort made in post-war years to increase output and raise the levels of living, most of the countries find themselves, nearly a decade after the end of the war, either with lower *per capita* real incomes than before the war or with real incomes which are barely at pre-war levels. In 1953 the *per capita* real income in Japan exceeded the pre-war level by about 5 per cent, but in Burma it was still 30 per cent below it. For other countries of the region, such as Ceylon, Malaya and Siam, the *per capita* real income increased rapidly during the Korean war boom but declined after the boom. The recent estimated increase in the *per capita* real income in India is due to a large extent to the poor weather conditions in previous years, which lowered the base for comparison. Taking the region as a whole and judging from the *per capita* production of food grains, the most important consumption item in the region, *per capita* real incomes are still probably below the pre-war level, suggesting a state of relative stagnation. Other evidence based on such data as are available in regard to consumption of non-food items also confirms this general conclusion.'

The report says that, as a reflection of the economic stagnation, there has been no marked change in the occupational distribution of the people. The great majority still depend on agriculture. Even the efforts to encourage the growing of commercial crops have not been very successful.

'The region is by and large an area of high population pressures and high density of population per cultivated square kilometre. Unemployment and under-employment are widely prevalent.'

In other parts of the world the force which has transformed economics, ended stagnation, and modernized human life has been the inflow of large sums of capital. But the report says that the inflow of private capital into Asia has very much fallen off, nor is there any likelihood of its early revival; in some countries there is a net outflow. The report makes some calculations of the size of capital investment which is needed:

'With a population of 1,200 million, increasing at an annual rate of 16 per thousand, the total net new capital requirement to maintain the present standard of living is $4,800 million per year, equivalent to 4 per cent of the total incomes. A rate of increase of 2 per cent per annum in the *per capita* income would require in the initial period a capital investment of about $10,800 million per annum, equivalent to 9 per cent of the total incomes.' The gap between these figures and the present rate of capital accumulation – probably less than 5 per cent in India – is alarmingly wide.

A prime cause of the poverty and stagnation is undoubtedly the population increase. The growth of Asia's population, the changing numerical balance between this and the population of the West, are decisive facts in the history of our time. In India the population grows at the rate of 5 million a year. Thus in the next ten years the increase will be equivalent to almost the entire population of the United Kingdom. In Japan the rate of increase is over a million a year. In Indonesia the growth is as striking. How great it is in China nobody knows, but the recent census figures suggest that it must have continued in spite of all the disorders in the country in this century. The Chinese Communists, following the Russian example, affected until recently to be unconcerned by the increase; once a country has adopted a Communist system it can provide, they say, for an almost limitless population. But they are controverted by all the evidence and there are signs that they have begun to recognize this. With increasing population farms become smaller, rents grow (where there is landlordism), misery increases, politics grow more tense.*

How to remedy poverty, how to end the squalor in Asia, how

* The United Nations survey points out that the rate of increase of population in Asia is not greater than in certain other areas, which are more highly developed. But the gravity of economic problems is increased more sharply in Asia than in these other areas, because Asia's population was already too large before the increase.

to give it the signs of modernity and prosperity evident in the West, have become the most urgent questions in the politics of all the countries of the continent. The concentration upon economics is relatively new; in the Indian Congress, Gandhi was the first to raise seriously the problems of the peasants' standard of living. For Asia it has been a new and startling conception that material standards can be changed by governmental action, but once the idea has spread it causes commotion. From now on no party can hope to have much backing which does not promise spectacular economic benefits, undertake to build great economic works, and to reform the social institutions by which the people feel themselves exploited or are taught to feel themselves exploited.

Land reform, the abolition of the landlord, provision of cheap credit, arrangements for cheap marketing, minimum wage laws – these are the currency by which the parties will try to win mass support. As a result, discussion among the political parties turns more and more upon the problems of national reconstruction. How is development to be financed? What is the role of the politician and what is the role of the civil servant? How can the goals of economic policy be properly determined? What are the priorities in development? From end to end of Asia these are the subjects debated.

The remedy for poverty which attracts to itself the most emotional force is industrialization. For countries whose rural populations are bursting at the seams industry offers hope; for the young man in the village, stirred by rumours of the new life, the factory is the way to an existence with greater opportunity; for the intelligentsia industry means modernism, national strength, and an abundance of jobs; for the politician and civil servant, industry means the source of revenue (from which social services may be financed) and military strength. Most of the national leaders in Asia desire to see the towns expanding in size, factories growing up in all areas, and huge industrial armies surging into being. The more intelligent among them recognize that industrialization cannot be a full remedy to poverty but only a palliative. However rapid the growth of industry may be, it cannot absorb more than a small proportion of the many millions of farmers who are already superfluous or keep up with the remorseless increase of the populations. Yet even for these, industrialization is a symbol. It means that at least a start has been made in social transformation.

This is the irresistible trend of thought of our time. One man, however, tried to oppose it, and for a time offered with success a counteracting ideal. This was Gandhi. It was a remarkable achievement of personal influence that he was able to fly in the face of the general impulse and for some decades confuse or weaken it. To Gandhi, and to some other fastidious reformers, the attendant horrors of industry were more obvious than its ultimate benefits. An industrial revolution suggested the conditions of early nineteenth-century England – the conditions described in the books by the Hammonds or by Disraeli in *Sibyl*; agriculture, however poverty-stricken, seemed to offer better prospects. At various times – though not always – Gandhi condemned, sometimes a little ambiguously, the whole apparatus of modern life – industry, railways, steam power, even medical science.

The fight of the Gandhians in India and elsewhere was in vain. The Asian towns might to a Westerner appear horrible – dreadful sites of poverty, slums, ugliness, class hatred, lacking in all the civic sense and graces and civilization which the West, with its Hellenic tradition, had tried, even during the industrial revolution, to conserve in urban life. Nevertheless the towns were what the peoples of Asia wanted. The towns grew. Gandhism could not prevent it.

To the problem of poverty Asia is now being offered two answers. One is the answer of Communism; and China is the country where the answer is being tested. The other is the answer of the controlled liberal economy. India is its chief exponent.

The Communists believe that the standard of living can be raised most effectively if society is treated as a kind of army and if there is a chain of command stretching from the very centre of the central government down to the humblest Communist 'cadre' in the village. Putting its faith in science and technology, the central government trains very large numbers of technical experts. One of the most impressive pieces of news from China is of the establishment of an astonishing number of training centres to which are brought many thousands of young men, the majority of peasant origin. With the technicians once trained, the government organizes them in the construction of large works which are meant to revolutionize economic life. Communism is pre-occupied with capital goods and is reluctant to indulge the population with consumer goods. The supreme aim is to develop heavy industry. The present generation must manufacture the apparatus of capital goods, which in theory will cause the future flow of enjoyable goods into the homes of its grandchildren. Communist man never is, but always to be, blessed: it is jam to-morrow, not to-day. Society is flogged along the way to better life not for itself but for posterity. What is the reason for this austerity? Partly it comes from the belief that Communist countries, being late starters in industrialization, can most quickly catch up with the more advanced countries by making these sacrifices in the present. Partly it comes from the resolve to amass military strength which heavy industry can give. Partly also it may be that to concentrate on producing capital goods is always the easiest way in economic planning; it involves fewer problems of adjusting consumption to supply.

Capital is needed in a Communist state no less than in a capitalist one: the difference between the two societies is in the manner of its procurement. It is the boast of Communist countries that they will effect their transformation the hard way by means of imposed savings. Capital is raised from the community by taxation, the regimentation of the peasantry, and the requisitioning of as much of the agricultural surplus as possible. This is probably the main reason for collectivizing agriculture. From a collective farm it is easier to collect taxes in kind, and the finance of the industrial plan depends upon the state taking from the farmer a much larger part of his crop than he would willingly surrender.*

The Communists, in spite of their general aim of maintaining

* Apart from this, collectivization in most Asian countries has little point. Their circumstances are different from Russia's. In Russia, where there was abundance of land, there was a case for making the unit of agricultural production a very large one and for mechanizing it. It might be hoped that this would increase production and economize labour, which could then be transferred to industry where it was needed. But in Asia, capital is so scarce that agriculture cannot be quickly mechanized.

secrecy about economic facts, disclose a good deal about the way in which their programmes are working out. A rather remarkable account of economic planning was contained in an article in the official newspaper *People's Daily* on May Day 1955.

'For the past two years,' said the article, 'we have committed the blunder of advancing blindly in basic construction and made the mistake of scattering our capital funds too widely, thereby jeopardizing the progress of the construction of key products. The construction of non-key projects still continues, and the phenomena of disorganized use and waste of state capital funds have become extremely serious. Personnel working in various economic fields still fail to establish a clear conception of cost accounting. Some comrades have taken the view that to achieve socialist industrialization, factories should be built without regard to priority or to whether the construction of such factories is in harmony with the State construction policy.

'The blind building of isolated industries is defeating the very purpose of industrialization and is resulting in waste. For instance, the construction of the Huangtankou hydro-electric station in Chekiang was launched on the premise that local water resources might be utilized. However, one point was overlooked. Although electric power would be available after the completion of the power station, the construction cost was so high that it could not be completed, even after more than 20 million yuan had been spent. As a result, it was necessary to suspend construction. Even so, the station still needs money for maintenance.

'Another weakness has been the concentration of attention solely on the building of new industries with a corresponding neglect of those medium and small industries already operating. Some comrades have paid no attention to studying whether or not existing factories could be used to produce new items needed by the state. For example, disregarding the fact that the electric wire factories in Shanghai and Tientsin already had a solid foundation, the Mukden electric wire factory has launched an expansion project; the completion of this will not only fail to utilize the equipment capacity of the factory, but would cause a surplus supply of electric wire products, thus forcing other factories to cut production. In this way, the accumulated capital funds become scattered, and the policy for their use on key projects is defeated.

'On the question of non-productive construction, a number of comrades hold the view that the construction of modern industry must be paralleled by the modernization of non-productive or welfare enterprises. Consequently the number of non-productive projects under construction does not harmonize with the current economic level of the country.

'All these facts explain that the problem of how to achieve socialist industrialization has still to be solved correctly.'

This is commendably frank. It is not surprising. What reason is there to think that a new, improvized bureaucracy, most of whose members have little experience, can make the decisions which will ensure a harmonious development of the different branches of economic activity?

The rival economic policy and answer to Asia's poverty is that of the non-Communist countries. This is the combination, on lines familiar in the West, of controlled free enterprise, with governmental action in shaping a general plan and in undertaking large works beyond the means of private capital. This system is not straight-forward 'capitalism'. The old categories do not really apply. To think in terms of them obscures understanding. The essential difference between the communist and non-communist economic systems is that in the non-communist economy freedom is not abrogated and the state does not have a totalitarian monopoly. The energies and enterprise of the people, as well as those of the government, are given scope and encouragement. Incentives, and not discipline, coercion and punishments, are the means of getting work done. The centres of economic creativeness are spread wide, over the whole community. Profitability, and not the arbitrary decree of a minister, determine – broadly speaking – the enterprises, other than the basic ones of obvious social necessity, which are taken up; and society is thus able to provide itself with an expanding stream of consumer goods. Trust is placed in the galvanizing force of capital investment – and the incidental damaging effects of this force are guarded against by social legislation based upon what was learned of the evils of uncontrolled capitalism in the West. If some of the governments of free Asia stress their socialism rather than their liberalism, this socialism is very different from Communism. They dispose of hardly any forced labour. They do not constantly infringe on individual liberties in the name of the necessities of economic planning.

The country which has most self-consciously practised these policies, and is regarded as a model and test case by other countries of Asia, is India. Since 1951 India has been operating its first plan of economic development. Even the most sceptical critics have been impressed by the results which are now beginning to be achieved. Agricultural output has increased spectacularly. (Partly this has been due to good monsoons rather than to governmental policy.) Irrigation has been extended. Industry is expanding.*

India's economic advance, and that of other countries favouring the same kinds of policy, have undoubtedly been very much helped by the Colombo Plan. The Plan has been much written about and its history is now fairly well known. It started in 1950 as a British Commonwealth venture. Its scope soon widened, and the area of its operations came to include most of South Asia.

It is not really correct to speak of the 'Plan' in the singular. It is a collection of the individual plans for economic development of the participating countries. The budget of the whole Plan – whose impressive figure of nearly £2,000 million is often cited – is simply the total of the budgets of all the individual plans. What has given the Plan a significance beyond merely advertising the national programmes is the arrangements for raising capital from

* Of course the achievement in India can be represented too glowingly. There have been disappointments. For example, industrial output has not increased to the extent which was hoped. There have been long delays in expanding the steel industry; investment in irrigation has been only half what was planned. Some economists say that India's rate of progress is slower than China's, others the contrary. (There are the same contradictions in the West in discussions about the relative rates of expansion in Russia and the Western world.) One view is that India can only make its full system a success if it receives much larger capital aid from the West than it is at present doing. At present India is receiving only $100 million annually from Great Britain under the Colombo Plan and about $150 million from America; it may even be a net exporter of capital, since it has been increasing its sterling balances. It could usefully absorb about $700 million.

the West to finance the projects. Economic stagnation in South Asia in the past three or four decades has been due partly to the drying up of the flow of foreign capital which used to set new enterprises in motion. One of the chief aims of the Colombo Plan is to revive the flow.

For preparing and executing the plans there is no central executive or permanent secretariat. Each individual country drafts its own scheme. Certainly the plans are discussed and criticized at the meetings of countries taking part in the Plan, and a certain uniformity results. Without the consultation, some countries might not have devised plans at all. Some of the national plans may be modified to dovetail with those of other countries. But the final decision about the projects to be undertaken, and their order of priority, rests with the individual governments.*

The part of the Plan which comes nearest to setting up genuine international machinery is the Bureau at Colombo which arranges for bringing Western experts to Asia, for exchanging Asian experts among the different countries taking part in the Plan, and for sending Asians abroad for training. The work of the Bureau in creating, by these different means, a supply of technicians is important because the lack of this class is a chief cause in holding back the pace of economic advance.

Nevertheless the Colombo Plan is in no sense an economic merger of the free countries. It expresses merely that they share certain general principles of economic policy. The question at issue is which principles will produce, in countries in which peasants are laboriously learning to be mechanics, the quicker and better results – those of Communism or of the Colombo Plan countries.

---

* The central body is called the Consultative Committee. This is a valuable new piece of international machinery. But it is not executive and it is not permanent. It is a gathering of representatives – sometimes ministers, sometimes officials – of the governments taking part in the Plan. It meets at irregular intervals, whenever the need for consultation is felt, and it surveys the progress in the area as a whole, discusses the relation of one plan with another, and debates questions of economic policy which may be of interest to some or all the countries. It is a very useful *ad hoc* body, but in no sense the executive organ of a federation.

PART SIX

Ideals

27   THE GREAT MEN OF 1955

In the eight years between 1947 and 1955, Asia had changed its leaders – not with a clean sweep but nevertheless significantly.

In India, Gandhi had been assassinated; Vallabhai Patel, the masterful organizer of Congress, had died. The older generation of Congress leaders by whom freedom was gained were ageing and one by one passing into the background. As they faded, more and more light fell on Jawaharlal Nehru. If he shared it at all, it was with a strange leader whom only India could produce, the man who disclaimed all concern with politics, though inevitably involved in them, the 'spiritual son of Gandhi', Vinoba Bhave. In Burma, Aung San, who had struck the note to which Burmese youth responded in the war years – uncompromising audacious nationalism – had died by violence. He was succeeded by U Nu, a man with a personality no less strong, but an apostle of Gandhian – or Buddhist – non-violence instead of force. In the other countries of South Asia the leaders came and went, sprang into world notice (assisted by their public relations agencies which the Asian countries had copied from the West), appeared now full of promise and now discredited – but none came near achieving the authority which belonged to those who really bestrode the Asian continent. Some were laudable and successful, like President Magsaysay of the Philippines; some had the secret of survival, like Pibul Songgram of Siam; but the present age in Asia would never be remembered on their account.

In Japan, also, politics were anonymous. Mr Yoshida, prime minister for six years, served his country excellently; but he never claimed or desired to be its spiritual guide. In China, Chiang Kai-shek is in decline, driven to Formosa, held up to scorn by all the propaganda instruments on the mainland of China, and by Communist parties everywhere, and probably already fading from the mind of the plain men in China. His adversity has been painful to watch.

> 'The agonizing shriek, the bubbling cry
> 'Of some strong swimmer in his agony'

He has made no concessions, and has thrown defiance at his Communist pursuers; but as time has passed him by, he can hope for no more than to depart with dignity.

Among the leaders of Communist China, Mao Tse-tung is pre-eminent. His picture is everywhere in China – gigantic portraits looking like a rather elderly woman, benevolent if shrewd. He is known as Grandmother Mao. He is a name and a face known in most other Asian countries even in the villages, because he symbolizes a movement and an ideal, even if one which is more dreaded than welcomed.

Nehru, Bhave, U Nu, and Mao – these are the four main figures in Asia in 1955. What do they stand for, and what kind of men are they?

About Mao Tse-tung, surprisingly little is really known. He is the son of a farmer of middle rank from the province of Hunan, which in the past century has produced some of the most assertive men in Asia. He gained his ascendancy in the Communist party because the tactics which he favoured – the organization of peasant revolt – succeeded when all the rival tactics failed. He appears to maintain his supremacy without much difficulty, in spite of ill-health. He lives in rather mysterious retirement in the Forbidden City in Peking, as did the former Emperors. For the world, he signifies the Chinese Communist Party, its programme, its menace, its materialism. He and the Party are one. It is hardly thinkable that they should find themselves divided. He is the Party incarnate. Without the Party Mao could not exist as a political figure. He is not an individual teacher or prophet, like Gandhi, even though by his individual idea he has caused the Chinese Communist Party to take certain courses rather than others. This inseparability of Mao and the Party gives him his strength. The allegiance given to him is that given to the Party, whose servant he is even though he dominates it. The civil war in China was fought between a party, of which Mao was the chief, and a personality, Chiang Kai-shek, who though the head of the Kuomintang, based his claim to allegiance rather on attachment to himself than attachment to any clear and coherent Kuomintang principles. China preferred a party to a person.

For Asia, Mao symbolizes the belief in the virtues of Communist party dictatorship, the belief that individual liberties and well-being are luxuries which cannot be allowed to stand in the way of the requirements of Communism, and the repudiation of everything in Asia's past which can be called unworldly or subjective. He is the hero of those who despair of tolerable life without revolution, and wish to see a violent end to most of the institutions of the past.

All the other three figures transcend party. Even Nehru, who is linked with Congress as essentially as Mao with the Communist Party, is thought of in the mind of most Indians as an individual dwarfing party, as a superlative figure, rather than as Congress prime minister. By his personality he has captivated the country; he towers over everybody else, and almost certainly will grow taller and taller with the passing years. India feels that his ideas come from his own inner being, and Congress acts most becomingly in being the instrument for their realization. He is the Congress leader, and is thought of as being so by the grace of God rather than by the grace of the party itself. Fortunately for the world, Nehru's views are those of an enlightened liberalism. He is eclectic, willing to incorporate in his programme the better parts of Russian or Chinese experience. But in essence he is the product of the liberal civilization of British India, and while he may be determined that his own ideas should prevail these ideas leave no room for the dictatorship of any party. With impatience he may take high-handed action in reorganizing India, but the ideal which he has in mind is of an India where the rights of individual men (with the exception of the individuals of a few over-privileged classes) are all safeguarded.

Thus, for Asia, Nehru symbolizes the belief that the Asian countries can be radically and adequately reformed by means of parliamentary institutions. By implication he symbolizes the rationalist and secularist attitude. However much he revered Gandhi, he has not been a Gandhi in politics.

By contrast the two remaining figures carry on the Gandhi tradition, though in different degrees. For both, personal ethics and the search for individual salvation have priority over politics, though they lead them eventually into politics. U Nu is a Buddhist, Vinoba Bhave a Hindu. U Nu is non-violent, believes in the sanctity of life, thinks that Hinayana Buddhism provides the means by which man may achieve equanimity. His behaviour as prime minister of Burma has caught the imagination because even while he has been engaged in civil war against desperate insurrectionaries he has refused to abandon his idealism in panic or because of apparent necessity of state. His often repeated and evidently genuine wish to lay down his power and retire to a monastery have reinforced his authority. Thus he has been able to shine like a candle in a naughty world. The relative tranquillity which has returned to Burma is in large part due to the impression which he has thus made on the country.

Lastly, there is Vinoba Bhave, in some ways an authentic figure of Indian tradition, in some ways an innovator. He is the sadhu, the religious ascetic who has abandoned all aims for himself in the world. In the past, holy men of this kind have usually retired to the Himalayas or the jungle to meditate. Vinoba Bhave's return to the world, as the disinterested preceptor about how it should regulate its affairs and how men should live in ordinary secular life, follows more the practice of Western mystics than Eastern. Gandhi, it is true, had acted just in this way, but he had been criticized by Hindus for doing so, and his concern with mixing religion with remedial action in the world was put down to Christian influence.

Vinoba Bhave has been internationally known for only five years. Knowledge about him is still nothing like as extensive as it was about Gandhi. Recently a study of his personality was written by Hallam Tennyson, a great grandson of the poet. Tennyson thinks him a much more intellectual personality than Gandhi. Following the Hindu tradition, he seems to have cleared his mind of all personal passion, and treats all mankind with equal charity. Gandhi, on the other hand, remained until the last a very emotional person. He thrived on affection. He reacted strongly against personal slights. Like Gandhi, Vinoba Bhave conducts his mission in a peculiarly dramatic way, though certainly it is not with a deliberate intention to be histrionic. He lives as frugally as Gandhi; he has no possessions except a watch and fountain pen and a pair of spectacles. Unlike Gandhi he refuses to travel by train. He spends his life walking from village to village, chiefly to exhort the landlords to give away one sixth of their lands to the landless. Like Gandhi he is attended by a crowd of followers – some of them idealists, some of them politicians, cranks, those in flight from neurosis, and connoisseurs of holy men. Among this retinue may usually be found two or three maharajahs. One of those who has given up the world to join Vinoba Bhave's mission is Mr Jai Prakash Narain, formerly the leader of the Indian Socialist party.

However successful his exertions may prove, it is not likely that Vinoba Bhave will procure enough transfer of land from the rich to the poor in order to solve India's land problem. His direct contribution to politics is limited: he has advised that the present Indian parliament should be liquidated as too sophisticated. But his influence is great; he appeals to the Hindu conscience; he is becoming celebrated throughout Asia, as Gandhi was celebrated; and if he lives he may continue to be a symbol of ethical ideals, of a gentler way of life, of an instinctive solicitude for the poor, of a challenge to all the vulgar ideas of the greatness of a government, which may prove a counter attraction to Communism and also a reproof to those who wish to counter Communism merely by force. 'The police,' he said once, 'are not expected to think out and institute reforms. To clear a jungle of tigers, their employment would be useful. But here we have to deal with human beings, however misguided. When a new idea is born, new repression cannot combat it.'

If it were possible to know how these four leaders would be regarded in a generation's time – Mao, Nehru, U Nu, and Bhave – that would supply most of the essential information about the course taken in Asia.

PART SEVEN

Asia and the World

THE competition between the different systems in Asia has been carried on in the shadow of the cold war. The great powers outside have tried to influence the result.

To some people in the West it has seemed that the non-Communist countries of Asia, though threatened by the advent of the new civilization in China, have taken a surprisingly cool attitude towards the solicitude of the Western countries to protect them. But the international picture was less clear-cut than it appears to these critics. The attempt to contain Chinese Communism has gone side by side with a continuing suspicion by Asia of the Western countries, who are suspected of wishing – or being impelled – to re-establish their former imperialist control in new and disguised forms. It has gone side by side with the long drawn out struggle of Annamite nationalism against the French in Indo-China, who did not withdraw voluntarily as the British and Americans had done. It has gone with pan-Asian feeling, which led all Asian countries to remember that China was part of the Asian continent. It has gone with continuing resentment against the West because the West had first used the atom bomb against Japan – upon Asian territory. Most Asians, ignoring the plain fact that the bomb had not been used against Germany because it was not ready, say that the West used its worst weapon against Asians, but had scrupled to use it against a European enemy.

The complicated international play between China, the rest of Asia, and the great powers outside is the spectacle which must now be described. Asian affairs have become a central part of world history, and this is a new experience for Asia.

A REVOLUTION in a great power has at all times of history caused disturbance far beyond its boundaries. For this reason, cool observers have usually watched the first stages of a revolution with alarm, even when the revolution is the result of an intolerable former régime; and for this they are often condemned as cold-hearted by the more idealist. When the second phase comes, some of the idealists change their view. This process has repeated itself during the Chinese revolution.

The tradition of China was one of a great military empire. The evil days on which it had fallen in the previous century were an aberration. When the Communist government came to power this was not widely enough understood. Because of China's long civil wars and the curious way in which some of them had been conducted, it had been taken for granted in the West that Chinese armies were rather comical; and it was forgotten that for centuries before China's collapse they had overawed Central Asia and on occasions had made audacious expeditions to such remote places as the Caspian Sea. But for this, the expectations might have been more disturbing and more exact. If a strong central government was restored, it was at least possible that it would try to recover for China what it would regard as its rightful place in the world. A rectification of this kind would lead to many changes in international relations and Asia would enter on a new period of change and tension. In addition there might be the desire of China to get even for a century of humiliation inflicted by the West.

China's renaissance might have been expected to have larger consequences because even in the quite recent past China's authority had extended further than the shrunken area which the Communists took over from the Kuomintang. Even in the nineteenth century, Annam and Korea had been tributary to Peking. These and similar territories on the edge of China had not merely passed out of China's suzerainty; they had become colonies of the West or had passed into the West's sphere of influence. The Chinese Communists might revive their ancient claims. Even if they did not do so, they might convince themselves that Western influence in their adjacent territories was a vital threat to the security which they could remove only by driving the Western countries out of the Far East. They were more likely to be persuaded that this was necessary because of their belief that capitalist countries itch for a war of intervention.

These were possibilities – which should, it is true, have been foreseen – when the Chinese Communists set up their government at Peking in September 1949. Within hardly more than a year, some of them had been realized. Chinese troops were fighting the soldiers of the United Nations in Korea, and a general war was freely spoken of.

America was the most immediately concerned and the first to take up the challenge of the Chinese revolution. This was not hard to understand, in spite of America's historical inclination towards isolationism. Because of its genuine and praiseworthy concern to build up China in the immediate post-war years, America had become intricately entangled with one side in the civil war, the Kuomintang. It had backed a loser; and by ill-fortune it was never able to write off its losses and to become disentangled. How extraordinarily complex was the development of its relations with China. As the news came item by item to America, revealing the deplorable failure of the Kuomingtang in the revived civil war, the American State Department decided at first that the best course was a quiet disengagement from manoeuvre in China. By stopping its promised aid to Chiang Kai-shek, it caused his prestige to fall more sharply, and may have helped a Communist victory. The policy may have been wise enough. But from the start it had been unlikely that it could be carried very far. In the mood of America, the charge that actions by the American Government had helped to spread Communism was a deadly one. A very large number of Americans were interested in China, partly because of commerce, partly because of America's great missionary and educational enterprises in the country. Thus after an interval, America's relaxed bonds with the defeated Chiang Kai-shek were once more tightly knit.

Chiang Kai-shek had in the meanwhile established himself on the island of Formosa. This was not the first time Formosa had been the last base of a defeated ruler of China; the last Ming emperor retired there when China was conquered by the Manchus in the seventeenth century. The geographical accident of the existence of Formosa was to have consequences for all the rest of the world. If it had been a smaller island, or if the Communists had at that stage possessed a navy or an air force, Chiang's career would have been ended in 1949.

From Formosa, Chiang, though shattered in prestige, could conduct a harrassing campaign against the mainland by bombing the ports and sowing mines in the shipping channels. This angered Peking, and, because of the increasing support given by America to Chiang, its anger was turned as much against America as against the Kuomintang. From this time on, Communist China's fanatical hatred of America, and America's reciprocal fear and hatred of Chinese Communism, dominated the international relations of Asia, and threatened to have consequences far beyond Asia.

The bitterness of the Chinese Communists against America must have germinated during their long years of hardship in the Chinese interior, when they were hemmed in in Kiangsi province, or on the Long March to the West, or living in the loess caves of Yenan. Cut off from the outside world, the Communists fed upon the dogmatic communist literature which explained China's troubles as being due to capitalist imperialism. America, as the greatest power of the capitalist world, was cast for the role of arch-fiend. When in the post-war period the Americans threw their support behind the Kuomintang, the hatred of the Communists became the more implacable; and when the Kuomintang was defeated, the Communists on the one hand refused to have any dealings with those who had aided them, and on the other hand were convinced that America would soon intervene by arms to try to reverse what had happened. Peking did not wait to see what America would do, but began at once aggressively to try to sweep American influence out of East Asia.

Americans were bewildered. They were astonished at the hostility assailing them from China; and they had some right to be so. Most Americans thought, without much self-deception, that their country had played in China the part of an idealist and philanthropist, anxious to promote the stability of the Asian continent and the improvement of its economic standards. This explained its aid to Chiang Kai-shek. Doubtless America in its actions was not guiltless of ulterior economic motives, but they were not the ruling ones. For years, while America was acting in this way, China has been more or less politely suppliant to America, even if there was an undercurrent of muttering and criticism. Then, with the Communist victory, all was changed. Americans found themselves no longer serenaded but the target of grotesque abuse. They saw Communism throughout Asia trying with some success to direct against America the very Asian nationalism about which America had been enthusiastic and which it had desired to foster. Ill will to China was increased by the reports of the ill treatment of American business men and missionaries.*

There followed a mass exodus of Americans from China. The turning out of the Americans from China was one of the major upheavals of the time. In the previous half century, America has permeated China in an extraordinary way. The coastal cities, like Shanghai and Tientsin, looked, at least in their wealthier parts, like American towns, and were full of American business men and American women. Large numbers of American families, coming originally to China as missionaries, had settled in the country. Now all the roots were torn up. Merchants, professors, preachers, journalists, administrators, lawyers, engineers, doctors – all departed. It was made plain to them that they could no longer conduct any profitable business, and that if they stayed they would be harassed, and might be in actual danger of imprisonment. There were significant arrests. The American navy was no longer there to protect Americans; it had sailed away from Shanghai as the Communist army moved in. Today in the huge city of Shanghai, only a handful of Americans remain.

America felt that China had betrayed it. A country which feels itself scorned and endangered acts under strong emotion, and

---

* Even if there had been no Communist revolution, China might have collided with America. Chiang Kai-shek's book *China's Destiny*, published in 1943, showed a very xenophobic spirit. His subsequent difficulty with the Communists made him dependent on America. Except for this, he might have turned against the West.

this was what happened in America. Its domestic politics were convulsed by the inquest upon what had gone wrong. Had America been powerless to prevent the Communist victory, or had somebody blundered, or, worse, had secret friends of Communism gained positions in the American administration in which they had been able to lead America into disastrous paths? Recrimination over these questions became an obsession; for the time being it made the fortune of Senator McCarthy. A kind of auction began in extreme anti-Chinese sentiments. For a politician to express level-headed views about what ought to be done might cause him to be victimized, and many found it unwise to say what they really felt. Strangely enough, the groups which remained the most moderate, and wanted a cautious policy, were the business men. They wanted peace, and were not uninterested in the possibilities of future trade with Communist China. But according to Communist orthodoxy, these men – the 'Wall Street gang' – should have been egging on all the others. This paradox has been pointed out by Mr. Owen Lattimore, one of the most distinguished victims of the hysteria which afflicted America.

Decisive changes took place in America's policy. One of its guiding aims from then on was to 'contain' revolutionary China. A consequence was a change in American feeling for Japan. It was necessary for America to find an ally in the Far East to replace China. Japan was at hand. Thus in an extraordinarily short space of time America passed from preaching to Japan the virtues of disarmament to exhorting it to rearm, from regarding the Japanese as delinquents to seeing in them the virtues which they had formerly looked for in China. America's post-war relations with China and Japan are surely the best example of the wisdom of the maxim that a country should conduct itself towards its enemies with the thought always in mind that they may one day become its friends – and towards its friends with the thought that one day they may become its enemies.

At this stage, in the summer of 1950, there began the Korean war. Its origin is still in some ways mysterious. It began with the attack by Communist North Korea against the South, but who instigated the North, and exactly what they hoped to gain, are not yet clear. Certainly on the Communist side the Chinese were not the initiators. Whether they were even consulted about the attack by North Korea is not known, though the probability is that they had been informed. For the first four months after the outbreak they remained surprisingly passive. But the war had brought back America into the centre of Asian affairs. Although a little before its start the American army had been advising the American government that Korea was not a vital American interest and was not worth a war, the government, to the surprise of much of the world, had decided that Korea was the test case of aggression, the case on which America must take a stand and resist and invoke the machinery of collective security, or else acquiesce in an enormous increase of Communist prestige and self-confidence. For those who thought in this way, the attack on Korea was similar to the German demands on Czechoslovakia before Munich. The fatal mistake in 1938 had been to appease. Therefore in 1950 America resisted and succeeded in securing the assent of the Security Council so that it acted with its mandate, and with the active support of sixteen of its members. Perhaps those who decided this action would have taken the same steps against the next major Communist aggression, in whatever part of the world it had happened. But as it took place in Asia, America became inevitably more closely engaged there than before.

The war began in June 1950 and lasted until the armistice in July three years later. It was peculiar because it was a limited war. Though America had taken the momentous step of intervening, it desired that its action should be confined to Korea, where the aggression had taken place. Already the horrors of the atom bomb had caused all countries to shrink as never before from the prospect of general war. Thus each step which America took was circumspect. Risks were run; but the guiding aim was that all the countries which were concerned with Korea should fight with limited forces, without the use of the new weapons and within the confines of Korea itself.

This strategy of America – together with the diplomacy conducted behind the scenes and the influence of other governments – certainly prevented a collision between America and Russia. But it did not in the end keep China out of the Korean war. In

November 1950 when the North Korean invasion had been repelled and the United Nations armies crossed the North Korean frontier in the endeavour to solve the Korean problem by unifying the country, the Chinese armies went to the relief of the North Koreans. Peking seems to have been genuinely afraid that a United Nations army, once victorious in Korea, would cross into China and try to put down the Communist régime. Its fears sprang partly from the world of illusion in which it lived, but they were increased by the reports of the sayings and ideas of General MacArthur, the UN Commander. In fact, MacArthur was under fairly tight control by Washington. But could the Chinese know that?

The Chinese forces which went to Korea were at first described by Peking as volunteers or irregulars, but according to General MacArthur they numbered nearly half a million, and comprised two out of the five field armies of which the Chinese army consisted. The war between them and the UN forces was savage. Intense fighting lasted for eight months; minor fighting for another two years. But though the forces engaged were large, the area of combat was still restricted (with small exceptions in air fighting) to Korea. Thus the war continued to be limited. This happened in spite of very strong pressure from a section of the American army and politicians for action by America against the Chinese mainland, which could be represented as America's best means of forcing the recall of the Chinese army from Korea. Fortunately the American government resisted this pressure.

The Korean armistice was at last signed in July 1953. America had succeeded in its main objective: it had frustrated the aggression against South Korea. But this was not the end of the struggle between America and China, which the war had set in motion. In the course of it the resentment of each side against the other had deepened. As each openly planned the ruin of the other, suspicion and fear increased. During the fighting in Korea the Americans had discovered that the atom bomb, on which they had counted to give them security and the power to enforce their ideas, gave them none of these things, for the conditions for its effective use did not exist in the Far East, and the bafflement which this caused added to the high emotions of the time. As a result America judged that its strategic interest required it more than ever to guarantee the protection of Chiang Kai-shek in Formosa. So, when the Korean war ended, the Formosa question succeeded it as the principal cause of tension in the Far East.

Peking's concern over Formosa is not always clearly understood. Why, it is asked, must it be so unreasonable? Peking controls the vast area of mainland China. Why should it become so excited over Chiang's continued possession of a peripheral island? If it was content to wait, would it not inevitably regain Formosa in the fairly near future, and without serious fighting? Chiang Kai-shek is not immortal. This was true. But Peking's interest was not simply acquisitive. It sprang from fears for its security at home. In spite of its spectacular victories Peking knows that there is still widespread dislike of its government. As long as an organized Kuomintang party remained in being, with an army and an administration, this kept alive the hope of the opponents of the Communists. It was a possible alternative government. True, the Kuomintang still suffered from the discredit of its past; but in its exile in Formosa it had undertaken a purge, and might seem to have been through a partial regeneration. In any case, the Peking government would not undervalue its possible effect.

This was the background of the long dispute over Formosa. Peking could not afford to leave Chiang to nurse his strength – or so it calculated. America could not relinquish such a strategic centre and such an ally as long as the danger of war with China existed. If war should come, it might be worth much to America to have on its side the Kuomintang organization. Thus the question of Formosa could not really be settled until it was decided whether or not China could live at peace with America, whether or not the Chinese revolution had started international convulsions out of which war must probably come, whether or not the Chinese Communist Government had expansive ambitions which must be combated by force.

In the last two years the judgement on these questions, both in Peking and America, has evidently changed from time to time. Immediately after the Korean armistice there were fears that the truce, instead of being the end of a phase of aggressive Chinese policy, was merely shifting the location of that policy. China had been contained in the north, but was suspected of moving its forces and preparing to break out in the south – in Indo-China, where the long-standing war between the Communist Viet Minh and the French gave it the opportunity for intervention. A crisis over Indo-China came in April 1954. The French had suffered the crippling defeat at Dienbienphu; America thought for a time of throwing in large-scale American forces to save the country from Viet Minh. Would the Chinese then intervene, as they had done in Korea? For a time the American government dwelt on the idea of deterring them by the threat of treating Chinese intervention as an act of war which would lead to war upon the Chinese mainland, in which the Americans would use the atom bomb. This was the time when the doctrine of 'massive retaliation' was prevalent. The popular view was no longer that world peace would best be preserved by fighting a limited war as in Korea, but that the limited wars, with all their dangers, might be prevented by threatening unlimited war.

The weakness in the reasoning was that it was not certain that China would be deterred. Atom bombs are not as terrifying a threat to China to-day as they may be in another decade or two when industrialization has progressed. Atom bombs can devastate an industrial or administrative centre, but in China, because the economic transformation has only begun, there are few such centres. What would be the military advantage of blasting villages and the countryside? It was rumoured that Mao Tse-tung had even informed Mr Nehru that it might be to China's gain if the bomb was dropped; little damage would be done to China's war effort, and all nationalist sentiment in Asia would swing to China's side and against America.

America's allies objected to radical action in Indo-China, and so, upon reflection, did Congress, and the thought of it was dropped. The crisis had, however, been so grave that all sides, seeing that the dreaded general war had been only narrowly avoided, took advantage of the international conference which had been called at Geneva to try to reach some accommodation. The Geneva conference was one of the most dramatic international assemblies of modern times. Though its original intention had been much more modest, it widened – though this was never officially acknowledged – into a meeting to examine whether the new revolutionary China could be persuaded to live on non-aggressive terms with its neighbours. It was the first confrontation at the conference table of Revolutionary Asia and the West. The psychology of the main participants, the atmosphere, the tension, fascinated all onlookers.

The irony of history was that those who had convened the conference had little idea of what they were setting in motion. It grew out of European politics – out of the tentative approaches by Russia after the death of Stalin for an agreement upon Germany. An international conference had met upon this problem, and though it had failed to reach any settlement, the atmosphere between Russia and the Western powers seemed a little better. It had been suggested, therefore, that if agreement could not be reached upon Germany, an exploration should be made to see whether there were better chances of agreement upon Asia. But to confer about Asia without China would have been absurd. Thus the Chinese Communists were invited to the conference, and this was for them a major triumph. To negotiate on terms of equality with Britain, America, and Russia, to be accepted as one of the great powers of the world, had been one of their prime ambitions.

The conference was attended by nineteen governments. It lasted three months. Nearly everything about the conference was badly reported in the Press and, unless future memoirs are vivid, there will not be an adequate record of its look and feel. Its upshot was a truce in Indo-China and the division of the country between a Communist north and a south which in part, at least pending elections, was to be non-Communist. There was no agreement over the conversion of the armistice in Korea into a firm peace. Formosa was not officially discussed.

What was the effect of these results upon the long-term duel between China and America? By most of the world they were interpreted as a success for China, a reverse for America. China had been able to dominate a major international conference. America had been persuaded to drop its plans for armed intervention in Indo-China.*

* America's dismay at the conference was shown by its refusal to sign the agreement upon Indo-China. But it agreed not to frustrate its operation.

These results at first spurred America on to still greater efforts in building up a defensive system against Chinese expansion. Safety for the world seemed to it to lie only in raising a new great wall of China – this time a wall to keep China from coming out. No sooner was the Geneva Conference over than American diplomacy started to build the South-East Asia Treaty Organization. This was to be a counterpart to NATO, which had checked the expansion of Communist Russia in Europe.

To many people in America the wisdom of this seemed self-evident, and a little earlier it might also have done so in many other countries. But a new situation was growing up. The Geneva Conference had started new trends which would operate for some time. The Chinese had become slightly less truculent; they seemed to be willing to negotiate; a growing feeling in the rest of the world was that it would be reasonable to allow them to do so. The sense of extreme military urgency faded out of the air. There was talk of compromise. Even in America itself the fiercest advocates of intransigence began to lose ground. Senator McCarthy lost his battle with President Eisenhower's administration, and this weakened the Chinese lobby. Perhaps the administration had been able to defy him because it sensed the weakening national fervour over the crusade against China. For all these reasons, the South-East Asia Treaty Organization, though it was eventually brought into being, proved to be a less formidable and impressive alliance than had been intended. Most of the smaller countries of Asia, which had been invited to join it, excused themselves, and it did not look a very warlike or frightening coalition.

The duel between America and China is not yet over. China still believes in the malevolence of America. It tries to marshal nationalism everywhere against America on the grounds that America is potentially the arch Imperialist. On the other side, America still believes that China is bent on driving the West from all Asia and fomenting Communism everywhere. America is not yet ready to abandon Chiang Kai-shek or to cease regarding the Kuomintang as an instrument which it may one day need to employ. It is still mustering its allies against China. But for the moment the conflict is being carried on more cautiously by both sides. Neither is excluding the idea of limited agreements – and out of limited agreements larger ones may grow.

The irony of America's policy is that America in its effort to contain Chinese Communism was constantly colliding with nationalism all over the Asian continent, even with nationalists who were entirely opposed to Communism. Impressed by the need to rally the small Asian countries against Chinese Communism, America has tended to scrutinize with too little vigilance the credentials of those who offered themselves to be its allies. It was already tied to Chiang Kai-shek. Circumstances led it to accept Dr Syngman Rhee in South Korea, who ran his country by very doubtful methods. It is allied with Japan; and though Japan was a partially reformed country, its reputation in Asia is naturally still suspect. It supports Pibul Songgram in Siam, who in the eyes of most of Asia is a more reactionary personality than his opponent, Nai Pridi, who had to flee the country and ended as a refugee in China. Sir Winston Churchill, explaining his alliance with Russia during the war, said that, if you were engaged in mortal combat with a tiger, and a crocodile offered to bite the tiger's leg off, you would not decline on the ground that you disapproved of crocodiles. In the same way America may justify some of its alliances. But the present is not wartime. Manoeuvres in a cold war should be different from those in real war. True, America had also some very reputable allies in South-east Asia. President Magsaysay of the Philippines is a model of a liberal-minded and efficient Oriental statesman. But the dangerous impression has grown up that the American wall of defence is being manned by many whose continued presence in politics does not conduce to the welfare of their countries. America, which once had been the natural supporter of most parties of protest and revolt, whose own government had been born in a revolutionary war, whose greatest names after Washington were those of liberators such as Jefferson, Lincoln, and Roosevelt, has allowed itself to become the patron and protector of anachronistic régimes.*

* American economic aid in Asia was before 1950 concentrated upon Kuomintang China, South Korea, Japan, and the Philippines. The rest of Asia was neglected. Since 1950 the pattern has of course changed. Aid to China has naturally stopped; aid to Japan has tailed off now that Japan has

It is this, more perhaps than any other cause, which has made America's policies so suspect to India and which has as often made the relations between America and India full of discord, misunderstanding and bad temper.

29 INDIA AND MEDIATION

INDIA at one stage believed it possible to hold aloof from power politics. But willy-nilly it has become preoccupied with the struggles between the Communist countries and the West, and particularly between China and America. After a modest start, India has begun to have a powerful voice in Asian affairs.

In America, India's policy has caused resentment, and also surprise. India seems by nature to belong to the Western camp, but it has dissociated itself from it with emphasis. In domestic matters India practises liberal democracy in an almost copy-book manner; it discourages its own Communists vigorously; and yet it seems, at least in American eyes, to thwart the building up of the system by which Communism in Asia could be safely contained.

India's involvement in the duel of America with China came about gradually. In the first period after independence India had desired to have as little foreign policy as possible. Its domestic

recovered its sovereignty. There has been a cautious beginning of aid to India. But American aid – given by various forms and through various schemes and institutions   has on the whole been conditional upon recipients being willing to undertake some kind of military obligations. A part of these funds advanced have been earmarked for direct military purposes. The countries which next to Japan have been the main recipients are Formosa, Viet Nam, Siam, Pakistan. American economic policy has thus had the unfortunate appearance of being an effort by America to buy allies in Asia, instead of being, as it undoubtedly was in Europe, an effort to assist in the economic salvation of the continent as a whole. The aid has moreover been given often to countries which are in a rather ramshackle condition, and has been used by their governments as a means of preserving themselves and of putting off the day for social and political reforms. America has thus been propping up its allies. It has not been building up healthy countries.

problems were urgent. It wished to live on good terms with all the rest of the world, being left free to devote its resources and energy to modernizing its life and combating its national poverty. In the first two or three years this seemed a reasonable aim. By contrast with Europe, Asia was a continent for the moment without much international tension; and even when the skies darkened and the struggles began, India still hoped to keep aloof from the troubles. Its government did not like Communism, but, following the liberal precepts of an earlier day – of men like John Stuart Mill – that a country had no right to interfere in the domestic affairs of another country, it had no sympathy with calls for an international crusade against Communism. As the conflict between America and China grew, India's chief desire was to be left out of it.

It could, of course, not live entirely secluded. In the winter of 1951, after the start of the Korean war, New Delhi received a shock when the Chinese Communist government restored its authority over Tibet. Forty years earlier Tibet had asserted its virtual independence from China, and the British government in New Delhi had regarded the maintenance of this autonomy as being of considerable importance to India because of Tibet's strategic position on the northern approach to the sub-continent. The new government of India was not willing to fight in order to prevent the Chinese from re-establishing their authority at Lhassa; but it took stock of its whole policy for protecting its borders. Before Indian independence the policy of the British government had been to maintain upon India's frontiers a row of buffer states which were independent but whose independence was tolerated because they did not align themselves with any outside power. Nepal, Sikkim, Bhutan–all Himalayan states – were examples; so on a larger scale was Afghanistan. After China's invasion of Tibet, India consciously revived this policy. In particular it showed growing concern over Nepal, where a revolution had overthrown the anachronistic form of government – by hereditary prime ministers – and had brought in a government which was expected to co-operate more closely with India.

In spite of this increasing caution, India was still resolved not to become entangled in the struggle between the great powers. It judged that the Chinese Communists had no territorial designs against India, at least immediately. It did not feel itself gravely threatened. Why, then, should it draw the lightning to itself by intervening in the quarrel?

This attitude of the Indian government was, of course, really the attitude of Mr Nehru. But his attitudes were also those of most of India. It was because he reflected them with much sensitiveness and accuracy that he attained his supremacy in India. The neutralist and pacific instincts were reinforced by the still powerful tradition of Gandhi. By its own liberation India had shown what could be done by non-violent means and it was unwilling to agree that Communism could be resisted only by force.

As the crisis in Asia worsened, Indian neutralism remained constant. But it changed in its expression. The Indian government became increasingly conscious that, if there should be a major international war, India, whatever its own decisions might be, was likely to become a battle-ground. Therefore it was not enough for India to stand aside from the conflict; it had also to take an active part in preventing the war from breaking out and in ending the crisis. Thereafter its influence was directed towards mediation. It offered its services whenever they could make international relations smoother. By its diplomacy in fostering the armistice in Korea, by the skill of its mission in Korea which supervised the release of the prisoners of war, by its part at the Geneva Conference (when officially it was not really a participating country), by its mediation over Formosa, and by its part in the work of the international commissions in Indo-China, India claimed that it had rendered services to the world so useful that the principles of its policy became clearly justified.

The visit of Chou En-lai to India in the middle of 1954, Nehru's visit to China, the part played by both at the Bandung Conference, and Nehru's visit to Russia – together with the comings and goings of Nehru's professional mediator, Mr Krishna Menon – all emphasized India's belief that it could part the contestants and keep the peace. So did its renewed refusal in 1954 to come down on the Western side and join the South-East Asia Treaty Organization.

India's objection to the American policy of containing China was based on more than the belief that the policy was more likely to end in war than in the peace which was its object. India disliked the American strategy because it appeared to be making use of Asian countries as a means to America's convenience rather than to be regarding them as ends in themselves. It seemed to be moving Asian countries about like pawns; and pawns do not like being pawns. The suspicion was summed up in the cry that America wanted to make Asians fight Asians for America's benefit. Who first used this phrase is not clear. But it had deadly effect, like the slogan in the war that Britain was ready to fight to the last Frenchman.

India feared genuinely that American policy would endanger South Asia's newly-won sovereign independence. True, India does not expect a revival of Western imperialism in its old form, but it is on guard against new and partly disguised modes. It fears that America, in its manoeuvres in the cold war, may end, even though without definite intention, in establishing a new control over supposedly free Asia as effective as the old imperialism. Hence India's outcry against any action by the West which seems to be settling affairs in Asia over the heads of the Asian countries. Hence its objection to the military alliances which America has made with Japan and Pakistan. They may not be India's affair – but they are the shadow of an infringement of Asian liberties. Because India's freedom is so new, India is doubly suspicious.

The Indian position has been stated very clearly in a memorandum by a cautious and experienced observer:

'Indians are deeply suspicious of alliances by which they will in effect be protected by the Western powers in the sense that nearly all the military strength will come from other people than themselves. They call it colonialism by the back door, and what they mean is two things. Firstly, a historical memory; the East India Company began by protecting native princes, and much of the European possessions in Africa began with protectorates. Secondly – and this is really a derivation from the first idea – they feel that if you are protected by someone you have to conform your policy to that somebody's policy. Indians feel that they would continually have to be adjusting themselves to what the Americans did or did not consider worth fighting for.

'If one assumes the likelihood of an immediate Chinese or

Russian attack, this is of course a quite unreasonable outlook; but Indians believe that for reasons of Russian and Chinese self-interest such an attack is not likely. Their attitude appeals to the deepest political emotion of the whole of South Asia.'

This means – and it is an unpalatable fact – that India, and other Asian countries which think similarly, believe that the possibilities of a revived form of Western colonialism are more real than the possibilities of Chinese expansionism. For reasons of politeness, many do not say this directly. But it is in their mind, and explains some of the otherwise puzzling things said on such occasions as the recent Bandung conference. These ideas may also be tinged by pan-Asian concepts which, though woolly and hard to sustain in the light of all the diversities of Asia, still make their weight felt. Many people in Asia have still an instinctive sympathy with China in its quarrel with America because China is an Asian country. With their reason they may prefer Western civilization to Chinese, but they have emotions also.

These ideas and the compulsion of events have thus led India to play an independent part in Asian politics, and this has incidentally produced some unforeseen results. India has been able to commend its ideas to the other countries of South Asia which formerly belonged to the British Empire (Pakistan dissenting however on certain important counts), and these, together with Indonesia, have created an informal block, conferring together upon international policy. The first meeting, called on the initiative not of Nehru but of Sir John Kotelawala, the prime minister of Ceylon, took place in April 1954, just at the time when the Geneva conference was assembling. Its deliberations, and the unity of those taking part, strengthened Nehru's hands in the part he was to play in the late stages of the Geneva conference. From the place where they first met, the group has become called the Colombo Powers. At their second formal conference they decided to convene the Afro-Asian conference which met in the spring of 1955 at Bandung.

There is surely significance in the creation of this group. With the exception of Indonesia its members are successor states of the British Empire in Asia. Under British rule, these countries acted naturally in unison in foreign relations, and this conduced to stability in South Asia. The Colombo block is an attempt to restore this unity in the changed circumstances that all the countries have become sovereign and independent not only of Britain but of one another. Because of their past association under British rule, they find it fairly easy to co-operate. The Colombo block is the ghost of the British Empire in Asia sitting on the grave thereof.

In the Colombo block, India is by far the largest and strongest country; the smaller countries are therefore naturally inclined to be jealous and to resent anything which appears to be dictation. On the whole India has been successful in lulling their suspicions and, in spite of mutterings and occasional threatened outbursts, in persuading them to work with it harmoniously. Some of them were less inclined than Nehru to think charitably of China's intentions internationally, and some would have liked to work more closely with America. But after frank debates they usually stood together.

With only one of the countries of the block was India on terms which were definitely bad. Its relations with Pakistan were the blot upon India's foreign policy. This followed chiefly from one cause, the quarrel over Kashmir. India's failure to accept the many reasonable compromises proposed by friendly mediators brought a nemesis. India forfeited a part of the respect which it would otherwise have commanded in the world; and Pakistan allied itself with America, bringing the Indian sub-continent into the middle of the cold war. By its intransigence over the small territory of Kashmir, India has thus endangered its world-wide policy. Mr Nehru's conduct is a remarkable example of how men of the most enlarged vision can bring their lofty aims into jeopardy by pursuing simultaneously those which are less high.

30   BRITAIN IN ASIA

BRITAIN was at first less engaged than America with the Chinese revolution. Though modern invention had shrunk distances so dramatically, the Far East still seemed far away, at least in the sense that Britain in the post-war period was not obviously involved there. Its connexion with China had actually become less than in earlier years, though it had still a heavy investment to defend in the coastal areas; in Japan it had surrendered all initiative in policy to America. Thus when the Chinese revolution happened, it seemed at the start to hold out no obvious dangers to Britain. Indifference was reflected in the remarkable failure of scholars in England to take interest in the changing situation in Asia. While in America a dozen research institutions, fairly well financed, chronicled and discussed the revolution, hardly a single book upon it of lasting value appeared in Britain.

In such circumstances, the instinct in Britain was to recognize fairly quickly the new Communist government in Peking. In this, Britain differed from America. But the British practice in the recognition of foreign governments differed also from that of America. In America, there was an assumption that to recognize a new government implied, if not moral approval of it, at least the absence of strong moral disapproval. In Britain it is accepted that the act of recognition has very little moral content. Recognition of a government is recognition of a fact. If a government has come into practically undisputed control of a country, that government is the one with which it is necessary to deal. Diplomatic convenience requires that it should be formally recognized. Thus it had been possible for Britain to recognize the Communist government in Russia in 1923, even though the majority of people in Britain regarded that government disapprovingly. Similarly it was ready to recognize the government of Mao Tse-tung. There was even a sentiment that what Mao had set up, though unpleasing in some respects, had many positive merits. The removal of the Kuomintang seemed to be a useful clearance. For decades, progressive people in Britain had been saying that they looked forward to a strong, stable and unified government in China. The Communists seemed more likely to provide it than their rivals.

Britain's recognition, which had been preceded by India's, was announced in January, 1950. For a brief moment it seemed that it might lead the way to an American recognition after an interval. But the results were not what Britain had hoped for. One reason for losing little time over recognition had been the hope that if friendly gestures were made to the new Chinese government, it might respond in a friendly way. It might decide that it was unprofitable to limit its friendships to that with Russia. On the other hand it was feared that boycott would drive China into seclusion. But the Chinese government, instead of showing the expected gratification at this recognition, took it very coolly indeed. It did not seem especially anxious to be recognized. Instead of exchanging ambassadors with Britain, it said that a number of points of difference must first be settled, and that the envoy sent to Peking could be no more than a 'negotiation representative'.

The points of dispute were relatively small. Britain, though it had withdrawn recognition from the Kuomintàng government, had kept a trade agent and consular representation in Formosa, and Peking objected to this; there were disputes over the ownership of Chinese aircraft which caused litigation in Hong Kong and led to anger at Peking; Britain had not sponsored Communist China's immediate admission to the United Nations. These complaints could have been discussed. But the Chinese government seemed deliberately to wish for bad relations with Britain. It set itself to squeeze out British business from the ports and to expropriate the British investment. The chosen means was to create the most vexatious difficulties in the way of the normal functioning of business. Workers, sometimes supported by the government, made extravagant and at times grotesque demands for arrears of pay. The movement of foreign business men was impeded at every step. They could not leave or enter the country without long negotiation.

In the middle of 1950 the Korean war began. This ended the hope of normal relations with the new China, and brought Britain at first into much closer harmony with America. The war was one of collective security; the principles of the United Nations were at stake, and therefore Britain, though it had still no particular feeling against Communist China, agreed to take its share of the war. At one time the British naval forces in the Korean waters were larger than the American. But throughout the three years of fighting, Britain fought the war less passionately than

America. It had far fewer casualties, and national emotion was less aroused. It watched the involvement of America with ever-growing anxiety. Its fear was that America might be entangled in a war upon the Chinese mainland in which American power would be employed at the greatest possible disadvantage. China, it has been said, is like a mass of cotton wool. You can penetrate it easily. But it suffocates you. Or it is like a great marsh. Suppose that this bog swallowed a part of the American armies, and drew others in after them, what then might Russia, freed from anxiety of American intervention, undertake in Europe? That was the thought constantly in the minds of British statesmen, both in the time of the Labour and Conservative governments.

The fears of Britain went further. It saw that a great danger to the West lay in a possible capture of the nationalist movements in Asia by Communism. Partially that is what had happened in China; the Communists had come to be regarded by many as better champions of the national cause than the Kuomintang. Many people in Britain were afraid that if America drifted into war with Communist China, nationalists throughout Asia would tend to sympathize with China because few Asians would really be at heart on the Western side in a struggle between a Western power and China. The Communists could use such a situation very effectively. They had already done so in miniature in Indo-China, where the French war against Annamite nationalism led to that nationalism being dominated by the Communist Ho Chi Minh.

In the later stages of the Korean war the difference between the British and American attitudes became still clearer. America became always more set upon containing China and building up against it a defensive wall by means of alliances. Britain was unwilling to see the Far East situation in such static terms. The whole of Asia was in a time of change. Nobody, it was felt, could see with any precision the international groupings of two or three years ahead. Britain wished to act on the old principle of treating its enemies to-day as if they might become friends to-morrow. The Chinese revolution was a complex event, with many different possible lines of evolution, and it would be some time before it was clear which line it would follow. Western policy might help to decide whether the line chosen was less or more favourable to the interests of the world. Perhaps the revolution would lead on, in the classic way, to ever more audacious national expansion; perhaps on the contrary, China's aims were limited; perhaps the energies of the revolution would exhaust themselves, and a new balance be established. If either of the two latter possibilities were to come about, war with China was unnecessary; and whether or not it was avoided would depend on whether diplomacy was skilful, and whether there was good fortune. In order to test the situation, and give the maximum chance to diplomacy, Britain desired to tie its hands as little as possible by rigid undertakings about the conditions which would provoke war. While it did not oppose the American effort to build a defensive wall – which was certainly the best deterrent to Chinese aggression – it prayed that its wall-building would be accompanied by supple diplomacy.

The British criticism of America has perhaps been rather smug because Britain has consciously – and it may be rather self-righteously – been following other lines, the chief of which has been the fostering of the Colombo Plan. Like America, Britain has believed in the virtues of economic diplomacy. Given the strained economic position of Britain in the post-war years, it has done a great deal – or promoted a great deal – with very restricted sums. Instead of trying to use economic power to shore up the weakest states in Asia, it has turned to what it thought to be the healthiest, or the ones with most promise, especially the successor states of the British Empire, and has tried to make these healthier. The basic principle has been that Communism in Asia is a product of economic distress and social backwardness. If Asia can be made up to date, the Communist danger will recede. Thus Communism may best be fought, not defensively by action against Communist parties or states, or by propaganda, but by concentrating on bringing about a rapid economic advance.

The sphere of the Colombo Plan was roughly all South Asia. Its central core was the succession states of the British Empire in Asia. There can be little question that the British economic efforts have helped to provide a sounder economic base, and on this the political successes in the region have been built.

In conducting its policies in Asia, Britain has been brought again into intimate touch with India. Of course there are differences of aim and of interpretation of world affairs. In spite of its present politeness and sentimental regard for Britain, India has not entirely forgotten the past; if it remembers with gratitude the British withdrawal in 1947, it remembers less liberal actions beforehand. Suspicion and dislike of Britain could easily revive. The Communists in India are trying to whip them up the whole time. In this century India may have a racial feeling against Europe as strong as European racial feeling towards Asia a hundred years ago. But for the present there is a remarkable coincidence of aim between the Indian and British governments. Jawaharlal Nehru, who would be the most alert to condemn this country if he suspected backslidings, appears now to regard it as a respected ally. The relations between British and Indian civil servants could not be more cordial. If British business men suffer from government action in India, it is not because they are British but because they are business men, and government in India has never loved business. After all, it was English civil servants who invented for business men the contemptuous name 'box wallah'.

Will the co-operation between Britain and India continue? India brings with it the so-called Colombo countries. Formally, India is still a member of the Commonwealth. It seems to attach value to the Commonwealth, and the exchange of information and views between Commonwealth members can serve it well. The Commonwealth bond would not survive a severe strain. But the London-Delhi axis is useful to both countries. It is a little more than an ordinary alliance. It is one of the most interesting uncertainties in Asia's future.

31 RUSSIA

ALTHOUGH the Communist victory in China had taken Russia by surprise, and although its past attitude to the Chinese Communist Party had been one of scepticism and suspicion, Russia could not fail to be satisfied by what had happened. Communist control now extended across a vast compact territory – all Eastern Europe and nearly all the northern part of the Asian continent. This was the area which some geographers had called the Eurasian heart-land. They had argued that if ever it was politically unified and economically developed, and if its economic power could be translated into armaments, the masters of the region could dominate the rest of the world.

That was indeed the long-term prospect which opened up when Mao Tse-tung set up his government. But probably Russia was more interested in the short term advantages. Traditionally Russia, like Germany, had had to fear being attacked by enemies both on the east and the west. The danger was at its greatest when Russia was invaded by Germany in 1941; if Japan had at that time attacked in Siberia, Russia might have been defeated; Japan's refusal to do so may have changed the result of the war. After China went Communist, this danger was almost eliminated for Russia. Its eastern frontier was splendidly guaranteed. An attack upon the eastern side would be parried by China.

These were facts plain for all the world to see. But in the first days of the Communist victory, it was still uncertain how close the Russo-Chinese collaboration would be. In Europe, the West had been gratified by Tito's break with Russia. That had come about because the Yugoslavs were nationalists as well as Communists, and could not tolerate the flat-footed dictation by Stalin. No people were more nationalist and proud than the Chinese. Therefore there were hopes that China would follow Yugoslavia's example. For many decades, the relations between China and Russia had been bad, and nearly all Chinese had grown up to believe that Russia was the mighty northern empire pressing mercilessly upon China's borders. It had to be resisted. During the Kuomintang period, Russia had practically absorbed large areas of the old Chinese realm, such as Sinkiang (for a time) and Outer Mongolia. Would it disgorge them, or would a Communist Chinese Government connive at their loss? By the Yalta agreement, Russia had been able to recover the privileged position in Manchuria which it had enjoyed before the Russo-Japanese war of 1905. Friction, perhaps a blazing quarrel, was expected between the Forbidden City and the Kremlin.

A few months after he had established his government, Mao Tse-tung went to Moscow for prolonged negotiations. This showed his skill in putting first needs first. It was his first visit abroad. What happened in the discussion is, of course, not known. But a treaty of alliance was signed. Ostensibly it was directed against fallen Japan. It provided that the one country would come to the aid of the other in case of any attack by Japan – or by an ally of Japan, which in the context clearly meant America. An interim arrangement was made by which Russia continued to enjoy for a time its control of Dairen and Port Arthur, but China's face was saved since it was specified that this was by China's grace and at its request. There was provision for Russian economic aid in the reconstruction of China, though the sum was surprisingly niggardly.

That was the start of the Sino-Russian collaboration. It has continued ever since. The West has watched minutely for the expected quarrels. From time to time it has comforted itself by detecting what it thought were signs that they were blowing up. But they have not happened. In its dealings with China, Russia has been as tactful as it was clumsy in dealing with the European Communist countries. Either Russia has not tried to interfere in Chinese domestic affairs, or its interference has been resisted and the conflict has been hushed up. Mao Tse-tung said, when he achieved power, that China had decided not to try to maintain impartiality in the struggle between the great powers of the world, but to 'lean to one side'. It has done so consistently ever since. It is symbolical that the new sky-scraper premises in Shanghai of the Sino-Soviet Friendship Association are the largest building in the country. Railways are being built between the two countries, and the bonds grow closer.

Not all the phases of Sino-Russian collaboration are an open book. The relations between Russia and China during the Korean war are a riddle to the West. Korea itself is an area in which both have an interest. If it was the Russians who provoked the war, as is generally supposed, Peking may not have been pleased at the prospect of an increase there of Russian influence. Again there may have been disagreement between the allies when the United Nations had repelled the first attacks in Korea and had broken the North Korean armies. It was believed in the West that Russia was in favour of abandoning the adventure, and it was said that China's intervention was made without Russia's approval. This may, of course, have been merely a guess. There is little evidence about what really happened. But once China was locked in contest with the United Nations, it could be seen even by the uninformed onlooker that Russia had a divided interest. On the one hand it was excellently served by a limited war between China and America. The American attention was distracted from Europe. By egging on China at vital moments, Russia had a fine card in the cold war. On the other hand, Russia, which almost certainly at no stage wanted full-scale war, was in constant danger that the limited war in Korea might get out of hand, and an uncontrollable audacity of the Chinese might involve Russia in a full-scale atomic war which Russia greatly dreaded.

Future historians may perhaps be able to reconstruct the complicated relations of the two countries during this period. A few facts are clear. The collaboration, whatever the strains, became closer. New negotiations led to new agreements. Russia's economic aid was enlarged. Though its aid in capital was not very large – certainly less than China's excessive thanks would suggest – it sent a very large number of technicians, and these appear to have given valuable service, and with rather less friction than has usually happened when Westerners have tried to advise Chinese. As the co-operation continued, the balance of prestige between the two partners changed. At the start it had been assumed that China's relation to Russia was that of a satellite. In fact, China seems never to have been treated by Russia like its European satellites. Before long, Russia was ostentatiously making China appear to be its equal. After Stalin's death there were further changes. Mao Tse-tung became the most senior of the leaders of world communism. His prestige exceeded that of Malenkov, and later that of Bulganin and Khrushchev. With this, China became in certain respects the senior member of the Sino-Russian alliance.

It has been surmised that this change cannot have been agreeable to Moscow. Moreover it was supposed that there must be rivalry between Moscow and Peking to direct Communist strategy throughout Asia. Who should guide the Communist parties in Malaya, in India, in Indonesia? Once again there is little evidence about how this competition has developed. It is known that in North Korea there was a pro-Russian faction in the Communist Party, and a pro-Chinese wing (and possibly a faction which was anti-Russian and anti-Chinese) and it is supposed that some of the purges in this party have been the result of struggle between the factions. Doubtless there are similar divisions elsewhere. But Communists keep some of their secrets well. They wash their linen underground.

What of the more distant future? The Chinese population already numbers 600 million. Apparently it is increasing. The Chinese government has introduced a conscription law. It is building a heavy industry. With the help of Russia it is building an atomic power plant. Certainly it will take some decades before its gigantic potential strength can be realized; but if its political system should hold together, and if its economic system should prove workable, China will one day be terribly powerful. There are few records in history of two great military empires living happily and peaceably side by side. The Russian statesmen, who to-day find China useful, must wonder what is to happen in the end. What thoughts passed through the minds of Marshal Bulganin and Mr Khrushchev when they were honoured guests last year at China's celebration military parades? Their uneasiness may be the greater when they recall that Russians are thought of by Asia essentially as Western people, that the Russian empire contains large numbers of Asian peoples, and that the vast wastes of Siberia, if mostly empty when they were overrun by Russia, are indisputably Asian territory. Will the Chinese tolerate the Russian intrusion into Asia when to an ever-increasing extent the history books of Asia represent the theme of this century as Asia's revolt against the West, and the rolling back of Western power. 'Asia has stood up,' says Mao Tse-tung. Will it not stand up for Siberia also, and for Kazakhstan and Tadzhikistan?

Communism is the bond which may hold China and Russia together. It is true that Christianity never preserved the political unity of Christendom. When Communism loses its quasi-religious fire and force, as it has already done in Russia (though not in

China) its capacity to bind may become less. Yet there will always be great inducements to China and Russia to stand together – so great that perhaps the result in the end may be some form of supra-national, supra-racial confederacy. What magnificent prospects must still dazzle any imaginative politicians in Peking and Moscow! Together, China and Russia hold the inner lines and can choose the time and place for action. On the outside are the lesser states as buffers between them and the other great powers of the world. In all these lesser states are disciplined Communist parties, eager to fight the battles of Communist world strategy. Directions from the Communist heart-land may result in an insurrection in Malaya, a political crisis in India, trouble in Indonesia or Burma. The world can be kept on the jump.

Of course the Communists are not always able to take advantage of their position. They may be clumsy, as they were in their recent intervention in Indian provincial elections. No elaborate machinery such as that of international Communism ever works with precision. That is one of the consolations of the non-Communist countries.

*   *   *

These were some of the international manoeuvres in Asia in the years after the Communist triumph in Peking.

Consider the changes which have been brought about.

What, in the broadest possible outline, has been the pattern of the events?

In 1947, Asia had been still only on the fringe of that part of the world whose events determined mankind's destiny. It was the suburbs of world politics, not the metropolis. Though Asia's vicissitudes might interest the outside world and compel its occasional action, and though its personalities like Gandhi might fascinate the West, they were still not felt to be central to world history.

The only action by an Asian people which was thought to have come near to deflecting the course taken by the rest of the world was that of the Japanese in building their empire and challenging America; but Japan owed its importance to the disturbed state of the world caused by Germany. In 1947, after Japan's fall, the expectation of Western man was that the previous conditions would be restored. Asia would revert to its subsidiary place. Though the changes coming over Asia might be interesting they would not affect Western man vitally. The assumption was that the fate of the West would not be decided on the plains of Asia. Events in Asia seemed therefore to be something outside the range of the truly momentous.

In Asia itself in 1947 a rather similar view prevailed, though it was expressed in a way less galling to Asia's pride. The predominant sense was that Asia was contracting itself out of the connexion with European and American affairs. Thenceforward Asia itself would settle the affairs of the Asian continent but would not intermeddle with those of the West.

These expectations, both of the Western countries and of Asia, were falsified during the subsequent years.

The world-wide cold war has caught up Asia; thus what happens outside Asia still determines Asia's fate. Here the hopes of the Asians have been confounded. But the West too has been forced to admit, however reluctantly, that from now on what happens in Asia may help to decide its own future. At times Asia has seemed to be the very centre of the cold war.

Thus the West, in a sense, is now Asia's prisoner, as Asia was the West's in the last two centuries. That is the fact which stands out from the recent events – from Korea, from the crisis over Dienbienphu, from the Geneva Conference, and from the long debates over Formosa.

CONCLUSION

WHAT is at issue is the form of organization of society in all the countries of Asia and the character of the men of the succeeding generation which will be formed by the institutions. It is a very great issue, for Asia contains a little more than half the world's population.

The history of Asia before the period of Western ascendancy had certainly been full of magnificence; but in nearly all the Asian countries the governments, though often splendid in appearance, weighed heavily upon their subjects. In the various desirable or profitable activities of life outside the narrow sphere in the villages the governments had a monopoly and discouraged or prevented initiative by private groups or persons, whether economic or political.

One of the achievements of Western influence in the countries which came under Western rule was to disperse this too much concentrated power and to permit private initiative. Out of this private initiative in the course of decades there grew up nationalism itself, the great political parties, such as Congress and the Moslem League in India, and impressive business corporations – banks, merchant houses, and industrial concerns – which, in imitation of those organized by the Western newcomers, developed not only in the hands of the Western intruders but of the local people. Such a proliferation would never have been tolerated under the traditional forms of government – of Moghul emperors, Burmese kings, Indonesian sultans. The state would have tried to deter, to control and to dispossess and, where it did not do this, would have taxed enterprise out of existence.

In China and Japan, though they did not come under Western rule, Western ideas of how society should be regulated were adopted at least for a time by the intelligentsia, though the ideas were not so successfully translated into practice.

To-day, in the countries which are the succession states to the Western empires – that is, in most of South Asia – the provisional form of society, the form which is on trial, is semi-liberal. Wide though the differences are between the succession states – reflecting different past histories as well as the different imperial influences which they recently came under – the states show certain features common to all. Opposition to the ruling power is tolerated. In all of them the scope and methods of government are defined, at least in a rough-and-ready way, by law. In all of them it is assumed that governments should be controlled and, if necessary, unmade by representative institutions. In all of them there is a constant debate between government and citizens, carried on by the press and other means; and the governments do not attempt, except in extreme emergency, to stifle the criticism. Opposition parties have rights and a definite part to play, and it is accepted that it is their legitimate aim to replace the existing government. Governments are sensitive to criticism and, if it becomes too scathing, may resign.

At present the system is functioning, though with many stresses, and more successfully in some countries than in others. Government by untrammelled nation-wide conversation – which is the essence of the system – is congenial to most of the peoples. But the future is uncertain, partly because the society, as opposed to the organization of government, is so different from that out of which the liberal institutions evolved in the West. Much is archaic and anachronistic; the centuries are jumbled together. The effect is that the majority of the people are uninterested in the survival or failure of the institutions – are not really citizens.

A Ceylonese student of politics, Mr M. A. de Silva, stated the situation very clearly in an article in the journal of the Hansard Society:

'Democracy implies the various freedoms. But freedom of speech does not mean much to the man who has never had the interest to attend meetings. Freedom of the press does not have much significance where most of the population is illiterate. Freedom of religion the average citizen in Asia does not understand;

he has been brought up in a tradition of religious tolerance. Appreciation of the right to vote requires a certain social and political consciousness among the people. But to most one form of government does not appear very different from another. They feel it will always be their lot to suffer in silence. Besides, they are also influenced by religious prejudices which lead them to think that one is governed by forces which are the result of one's own actions in this and previous births.'

This is the context, says Mr de Silva, of liberal democracy in Asia. One of the chief impediments to the success of the system is the absence of a public opinion which could put a check upon the unscrupulousness of the totalitarian parties in using every means to wreck the liberal system.

'The enemies of democracy enter the legislatures not to work them but to destroy them from inside,' says Mr de Silva. 'Their only interest in Parliament is to make use of it as a forum from which to broadcast their anti-democratic views. Under the safety of the privileges of parliament, the most wicked and malicious attacks can be made on public servants. Innuendo is the most formidable weapon in the totalitarian armoury.'

Until these conditions change – as a result of education or social advance – the liberal part of Asia will continue to be in a state of siege, and situations will continue which are potentially revolutionary. But revolution, if it does occur, will not be on the pattern described by Karl Marx. Seizure of power by the proletariat in order to govern in the interest of the whole proletariat is one of the romantic concepts of nineteenth-century Europe, certainly not destined to be realized in twentieth-century Asia. Revolution will be made by organized groups bent on seizing power for its own sake, using whatever grievances exist in society as a means of battering their way to power and of overthrowing the existing system. Revolution made by an authoritarian party of the right may in certain circumstances be as likely as one made by a party of the left. Revolution does not necessarily mean Communism.*

* Acute analysis of the nature of revolutionary situations in under-developed countries has been made recently by Professor R. W. Seton-Watson. He has shown how little the picture of Asia to-day, though genuinely revolutionary, corresponds with the picture given by Karl Marx.

But if one of the threats to the liberal civilization may in future come from parties of the right – probably Chauvinists and extreme nationalists – at the present time the main existing threat is from Communism. Communist China is the great example of the Asian society which, having tested liberalism, has renounced it.

The Chinese revolution is a very great event, the product of great hopes and idealism, and it is easy to be swept off one's feet in contemplating it. The wrongs out of which it grew were shocking. Every exact picture of traditional China shows, even in quiet and more prosperous times, the mass of people living in dreadful poverty, and, worse, being made poorer – thrust down below an already intolerable level – because they were preyed on by those who enjoyed either political or economic power. It was not only the larger exploiters who made life miserable – great landlords (of whom there were very few), tyrannical magistrates – but the petty exploiter, himself exploited, who wrung out of those below him a percentage of their miserable income. Traditional China was a land of hungry farmers, driven from time to time by land shortage and by the evils of social organization to final despair and banditry. Even Kuomintang China, where reform received at least mouth honour, was little better. Let its picture – the picture of the dying bird – be remembered. Rack-rented peasants, gross levies by moneylenders, conscripts swept off from their homes in chains, discontented and unemployed students, an intelligentsia without a faith except to condemn the existing system, an encouragement by the government for the out-of-date in ideas and culture, a disordered currency, a government apparently powerless to bring the aid of modern science to protect the peasant against nature, endless war and pillage by soldiers, an official life in which the corrupt and the elderly flourished best and got the rewards, humiliation from the resident foreigner – that was what the Communist revolution aimed at subverting.

Communism, seen in one light, is an effort by a group of the intelligentsia, inspired by moral ideas borrowed from the West – and also by an inaccurate interpretation of history also borrowed from the West – to end or lessen the exploitation, to see that more justice was done to the mass of the people, and to open to them the opportunities of better life made possible by science. It

211

can seem an exhilarating spectacle; and since many of the evils which breed Communism in China are to be found in the other main societies in Asia, it is possible that they also will follow Asia's course.

The tragedy lies in where the course leads. Communism may begin in a moral aspiration, but it ends in the tyranny now established in China. It becomes a social and political system, served and supported by all kinds of men and classes who were untouched by its moral appeal, but who found it prudent or necessary or natural to conform. It becomes a rigid system with its own vested interests.* With this it may lose its force and fervour and capacity to work changes, and may undergo various modifications. Some of the institutions which constitute it may be good. But on balance and in the end it is a system inferior to the new liberal system (even with all its present shortcomings) of the non-Communist countries of Asia, assuming that this system can survive and endure. Within the Communist system there is less freedom, less employment of reason, less originality of idea, less elasticity, and also, if the liberal systems are able to effect the transformation they are aiming at, in the end less equality and social justice.

This does not mean that the better system will necessarily prevail. A vast propaganda is engaged in making the worse appear the better cause. A formidable amount of emotion and interest are enlisted on the Communist side. Communism offers, delusively but plausibly, a sudden transition to a better life, and not a period of slow improvement, making heavy demands on patience. It appeals to youth, and it claims to be allied with science. The fact that the anti-liberal cause is now represented in such a mighty country as China, which may appear to be justifying its cause by success, naturally worsens the prospects of liberalism in Asia. If China's prestige grows, rival ideals may be in eclipse. Moreover, China's active aid to Communist parties in Asia, and the possible threat ultimately of the support of Communism by Chinese armies, weight the balance. Anti-liberalism may become a crusade, carried on with immense material power.

Certain historical circumstances may, however, help to save at

* The same happened with Christianity and Islam.

least a part of free Asia, especially India, from accepting China as an example. In India, Hinduism is still a tremendously strong tradition; if Indian society is reformed of its archaic excesses, Hinduism itself – or its basic concepts – may be strengthened because they will be less assailable. From the earliest days of Indian history Hindus have been concerned about the state of the individual human soul and have been hungry for individual salvation. In the course of centuries they constructed sweeping metaphysical doctrines, some of which had as their base the belief that the world was in a sense illusory and that salvation was to be found by withdrawal, others the idea that salvation was to be found by action in the world. But whichever doctrine was accepted the emphasis was on personal salvation; each man had to live his own life and determine his fate by his own decisions; the drama of the individual human soul was, morally and metaphysically, of infinitely more emportance than the vicissitudes of empires and the fate of mankind in the mass; these were but the setting, tremendously spectacular though they might be, for the personal drama. The great images of traditional Hindu thought – the images of the sadhu meditating on the mountain-side, of the Brahmin living in the world but without attachment to the world, of the warrior who fights because it is the predestined duty of his life, and all these and other castes by their different means striving to find salvation and peace – still live powerfully in the Hindu mind. While they do so it will be difficult to enclose India within a Communist strait-jacket.

In China the historical tradition was much more favourable to Communist totalitarianism. In some respects the new China is the old China distorted and elaborated. For in China government has always been carried on by a bureaucracy versed in a national scripture and using all the instruments of propaganda to maintain its authority. Communism has replaced Confucianism. The extreme concern about indoctrination, the drilling of the population by innumerable meetings for studying the Communist scriptures, are the attempt to make Communist ideas as pervasive and unquestionably accepted as were the Confucian ones. Moreover, in China there did not exist, except perhaps among some sects of Buddhists, the same passionate spiritual individualism as in India.

Men were content to observe the rites approved of by the government. They were not greatly interested in religion. 'Revere spirits but keep them at a distance,' said Confucius. A society thus disposed was not likely to resist Communist secularism very strongly.

With the lapse of time, Communism in China may lose some of its aggressive impetus, and the pressure on the non-Communist world may thus be relieved. Revolutions after a time lose their vitality, and cease to be an international danger. In Russia there are signs – perhaps deceptive – of revolution petering out; China, which borrowed its doctrine from Russia, may reflect the change. But it is too early to know. For the present the revolutionary fires are still burning.

The Chinese and Indian experiments are both deeply influenced by ideas and models in the West, but the Chinese and Indians have no unshakable loyalty to these. In the end their attitude is pragmatic; they will accept whatever system of government proves best able to make their countries strong and up to date. To modernize Asia is the aim above all others. It is necessary to remember this always, and to remember also the impediments. The spectacle of Asia is of peoples, the greater part of whom are peasants, being organized painfully to run industry, to run a complex modern administration, to serve in modern armies. All the old institutions which stand in the way must go – anachronistic divisions within society, caste distinctions, old attitudes of mind which shrank from activity in the world, the joint family, the seclusion of women, the moral values of a stable agrarian society. Asia is to become a continent of industrial cities, universal literacy, vast conscript armies, rapid means of communication and, if possible, material wealth. Whatever system of state can offer the hope of the quickest transformation will enjoy the most prestige.

The future in Asia is extremely hard to predict. It depends on too many ever-changing circumstances. Accident and the chances of personality will play their part. War would, of course, transform all; so might the appearance in Asia of some single demoniac personality, an Asian Hitler or Stalin, a new Chinghiz Khan of the atomic age. New inventions may in a lifetime utterly change all the conditions of life and alter all the present forces. Quite new political systems may result. With the whole world changing with amazing speed, Asia is caught up in the changes.

Who can foretell what further and yet more radical changes may come about from the introduction of atomic power? India, China, and Japan are all experimenting with its use. Every major innovation in the means of economic production has in the past started major political upheavals; the Industrial Revolution is the obvious example. If atomic power is harnessed, the changes which it may bring about in Asia may surpass those brought about by gunpowder, steam, and electricity.

At present it might seem that the supreme and most sinister force likely to be at work in Asia in the next half century will be that of the pressure of population. China has already nearly 600 million people, and their increase may strengthen the tendency of the Chinese revolution to end in an enlargement of the Chinese empire, India has nearly 400 million, and the population grows at the rate of 5 million a year. Population pressure may be invisible but is remorseless, and its results may be visibly devastating. An unchecked population may drive any country to revolution, upheaval, expansionism and yet more revolution, however good its original institutions. Yet nobody can foresee even these trends with certainty. Population scares in the past have passed without harm, though some population crises have been real enough. With industrialization the birth-rate usually falls (though the death-rate may do so even more, and an increase of population may thus for a time continue). Birth-control, if cheap and practicable means can be propagated, might alter all the economic problems of Asia; a small beginning has been made in India, and the opposition has been less than was expected. The economic changes in the world may be such that food and work can still be found. Agriculture in many countries is so backward that striking improvements of output are quite possible.

The greatest uncertainty of all is the future of religion. In a long survey of history, religion is one of the main forces shaping man. Burckhardt analysed all history into that of the state, of society, and of religion. The present age is secular, even in Asia; yet it is unlikely that man is changing his nature or that Burckhardt's analysis will in future contain one factor too many. Communism itself, though now atheist, engages some of the emotions of religion, and may in future become more involved with them. Nothing has brought so many surprises, so many alterations in world history, as new religions which attain large followings, and often their appearance is entirely unforeseen. Who in the year A.D. 600 could have surmised that a new world religion would spring from the deserts of Arabia and that in a century and a half it would sweep away much of the Byzantine empire, threaten western Europe, and send its missionaries to India and China? Who can be certain that Asia, which has fostered the great religions, is now barren, and that it will continue for long to admire and imitate the secularism of the West? Or that Communism, at least in its present form, will prove a lasting substitute for a true religious faith?

EPILOGUE

In the year 1926 an international conference on world peace was held at Bïerville. It was organized chiefly by Frenchmen and Germans. But it was attended by a number of Asians, some of whom were later to play a part in the liberation of their continent. A group of these submitted to the conference a memorandum which expressed very well the sentiments of the young nationalists of Asia thirty years ago. The signatories included Dr Mohammed Hatta, now Vice-President of Indonesia, and Sardar K. M. Panikkar.

'There is one thing,' said the memorandum, 'which cannot fail to strike anyone who studies the peace movements of Europe. It is the fact, which even your deliberations to-day have emphasized, that when European people think of peace they think of it only in terms of Europe. In the imagination of European thinkers the world seems to be confined to the areas inhabited by European races. The vast continent of Asia, containing some of the most ancient civilizations, and holding the vast majority of the human population, and Africa, with its particular problems, do not seem to come into the picture at all. This, we submit with all humility, is a wrong point of view. If the world is to have permanent peace it must not be a local peace, a peace affecting only a few nations, but must extend its beneficent reign over the whole of human kind.

'To our European friends of peace, the raid of a few irregulars into the territory of Yugoslavia is of greater importance than a war in Mecca.

'The subjection of Asiatic peoples – of the population of India, Egypt, Indo-China, and Indonesia – the economic and political subordination of China – are all a menace to lasting peace. The shadowy peace which foreign governments establish by the force of their bayonets is no peace at all. It is merely peace by terrorism. Such a peace is worse than war, because it raises in the hearts of men hatred – blazing, uncontrollable hatred – which some time or other is likely to burst out. All have noticed how the European is hated throughout the East. Why? Is it because the Asiatics – the Chinese, the Indians, or the Egyptians – are a barbarous people? No; but because all over Asia we feel that we are being held down mercilessly by the force of superior arms. Is this accumulation of hatred an asset for peace, or is it its greatest enemy? If you wish for peace, your first work should be to eliminate the causes which make Asia hostile towards Europe and to dissolve this vast accumulation of hatred. Establish a brotherhood of co-operation between Asia and Europe, and you would have taken the biggest step towards peace.

'Let it not be forgotten that a progress which excludes the vast majority of human beings, and affects only a fraction, can never be permanent. Can it be that Europe can progress without Asia? Can it be that whatever progress is so achieved by the unaided efforts of Europe can be safeguarded without the co-operation of Asiatic people? Let China, India and the rest of Asia be free. Then you would have built up a family of freed people willing to live together in co-operation. More than that, you would have eliminated the most potent causes of war.'

That was written in 1926. Twenty-nine years later China, India, and nearly all the rest of Asia were in fact free; the family of freed peoples existed; raids in Yugoslavia no longer eclipsed all the news from the East; but, alas! not all the results promised had come about.

In April 1955 another international conference took place whose object was once more the search for means of safeguarding peace. This conference was on Asian soil, at Bandung, in the former Dutch colony of Indonesia. Delegates from twenty-nine Asian and African countries attended. A few of those who had been present at the Bierville conference came to Bandung also.

The conference has a curious origin. It had been proposed several months earlier by Mr Sastraomidjojo, the Prime Minister of Indonesia. For various reasons, Indonesian nationalism had accepted less easily than other Asian nationalists the fact that Western imperialism was at an end, and it wished for an Asian demonstration to affirm once again its wickedness. Moreover, Africa was to be emancipated as well as Asia. Other Asian countries saw advantage in an Asian conference and accepted the invitation. Once the conference was mooted it was hard to be selective about those invited. Israel, it is true, was ruled out, because if it had come all the Moslem nations would have declined. But a very varied assemblage was selected. The Turkish, Japanese, Ethiopian, and Gold Coast governments were all brought in. Even the ex-Mufti of Jerusalem and the Ethnarch of Cyprus attended in their personal capacities. But no agenda was prepared in advance. Delegates arrived therefore in a state of some uncertainty about what business was to be transacted.

Partly the conference resolved itself into a demonstration that Asia really was independent, and that the Asian countries were not only free to live their own lives but were conferring on the great questions of the world and, as citizens of the international community of nations, were exercising their influence on the settlement of world quarrels. The debates were responsible and informed. They sent up the prestige of the Asian countries, and as a result the Asian countries gained in self-confidence.

Partly the conference turned into a full-scale analysis of the greatest question before Asia to-day, the relations between China and the rest of the continent. In turning to this question the conference showed its vitality. To condemn Western colonialism was a habit acquired from the past; to grapple with the problem of China was a matter of the present. Chou En-lai attended the conference. For five days the countries of Asia which feared Communism expressed their apprehensions about China's plans. A new Communist imperialism by China had replaced the old Western imperialism as a main danger in Asia.

Chou En-lai dealt with the attacks with skill and dignity. He would not be drawn. He would not retort. He would not justify China. He breathed friendliness and conciliation. He was ready to settle with any Asian country the status of overseas Chinese, disputed frontiers, and any other matters which caused friction with China. He was affable and approachable. He used the conference as a platform for offering to negotiate with America over Formosa and thus to relieve world tension, which would be very much to the advantage of all China's critics.

Chou in fact could hardly have been more conciliatory; he made the impression he wished and half won over some of China's critics. Yet when the conference broke up it was clear to everybody that the problem of how the rest of Asia was to live with China had become a prime one for the continent. The old disputes were sinking back into the past. The old scenes and enthusiasms appeared out of date.

Chou En-lai debating with the prime ministers of Asia was the significant picture, the living picture of to-day. Times had changed. The jubilation of the Delhi parliament in August 1947 was a picture which belonged to the galleries of history. The age of imperialism seemed already remote: that was why the oratory at the conference, denouncing the poor remains of Western rule – Goa and New Guinea – had seemed old-fashioned. Even the concept of Asia had begun to dissolve; what had created 'Asia' was opposition to the West. But the new age had brought new concepts and new groupings; and of these the one most clearly defined was the grouping on the one side of the Communists, on the other of the countries which still believed in the value of the individual human being and the necessity for individuals to be permitted to decide their own fate and that of their societies by free choice.

In the light of this conflict the old preoccupation with the upsurge of Asia against the West appeared already obsolete. Nevertheless its aftermath is bound to last for decades and to become mixed with and to influence the result of the struggles of the present day.

DATES OF IMPORTANT EVENTS

1857	Indian Mutiny
1868	Meiji Restoration in Japan
1904–5	Russo-Japanese War
1911	Fall of Manchu Empire in China
1919	Montagu-Chelmsford Reforms in India
	Beginning of dyarchy
1922	Formation of Chinese Communist Party
1925	Death of Sun Yat-sen
1926–8	Northern expedition of Chiang Kai-shek
	Kuomintang government established at Nanking
	Revolt by the Communists
1931	Japanese aggression in Manchuria
1935	Government of India Act establishing popular government in provinces, and providing for dyarchy in a federal central government
1937	Beginning of Sino-Japanese War
1941	Pearl Harbor
1942	Congress 'open rebellion' in India
1945	Dropping of atom bomb at Hiroshima and surrender by Japan
1946	Cabinet mission in India. Communal tension. Philippines independent
1947	14 August Pakistan independent
	15 August India independent
	Renewal of civil war in China between Kuomintang and Communists

1948	January	Burma independent
		Assassination of Gandhi
	August	Death of Jinnah
		Battle of Hsuchow
1949		Communist government proclaimed at Peking
		Dutch recognize independence of Indonesia
1950		Indian constitution comes into force
		India a republic
		Outbreak of Korean War
1951		San Francisco Peace Treaty with Japan
		Indian general elections
1953		Armistice in Korea
1954		Battle of Dienbienphu
		Geneva conference
		Formation of S.E.A.T.O.
1955		Bandung conference